The Girl with the Green Eyes

Clyde Fitch

Contents

THE GIRL WITH
THE GREEN EYES

BY

Clyde Fitch

To
CLARA BLOODGOOD

Good Friend and Ideal Interpreter
of "Jinny"

THE GIRL WITH THE GREEN EYES

The Persons More or Less Concerned in the Play

"JINNY" AUSTIN.
MR. TILLMAN } *Her Parents.*
MRS. TILLMAN }
GEOFFREY TILLMAN. *Her Brother.*
SUSIE. *Her Cousin.*
MISS RUTH CHESTER }
MISS GRACE DANE } *Her Bridesmaids.*
MISS BELLE WESTING }
MISS GERTRUDE WOOD }
MAGGIE. *Maid at the Tillmans'.*
HOUSEMAID. *At the Tillmans'.*
BUTLER. *At the Tillmans'.*
FOOTMAN. *At the Tillmans'.*
JOHN AUSTIN.
MRS. CULLINGHAM.
PETER CULLINGHAM. *Her Son.*
MRS. LOPP.
CARRIE. *Her Daughter.*
A FRENCH COUPLE.
A GERMAN COUPLE.
A GUIDE.

A DRIVER.
A GROUP OF TOURISTS.

Originally produced under the management of Charles Frohman at the
Savoy Theatre, New York, on the 25th of December, 1902, with the
following cast:--

"Jinny" Austin	Miss Clara Bloodgood
Mr. Tillman	Mr. Charles Abbott
Mrs. Tillman	Mrs. Harriet Otis Dellenbaugh
Geoffrey Tillman	Mr. John M. Albaugh, Jr.
Susie	Miss Edith Taliaferro
Miss Ruth Chester	Miss Lucille Flaven
Miss Grace Dane	Miss Mary Blyth
Miss Belle Westing	Miss Helena Otis
Miss Gertrude Wood	Miss Felice Morris
Maggie	Miss Lucile Watson
Housemaid	Miss Angela Keir
Butler	Mr. Gardner Jenkins
Footman	Mr. Walter Dickinson
John Austin	Mr. Robert Drouet
Mrs. Cullingham	Mrs. McKee Rankin
Peter Cullingham	Mr. Harry E. Asmus
Mrs. Lopp	Miss Ellen Rowland
Carrie	Miss Clara B. Hunter
A French Couple	{ Mr. Henry De Barry
	{ Miss Louise Delmar
A German Couple	{ Mr. J. R. Cooley
	{ Miss Elsa Ganett
A Guide	Mr. Frank Brownlee
A Driver	Mr. Lou W. Carter

	{ Miss Elizabeth French
A Group of Tourists	{ Miss Gertrude Bindley
	{ Miss Myrtle Lane

ACT I

A charming room in the Tillmans' house. The walls are white woodwork,
framing in old tapestries of deep foliage design, with here and there
a flaming flamingo; white furniture with old, green brocade cushions.
The room is in the purest Louis XVI. The noon sunlight streams through
a window on the left. On the opposite side is a door to the hall. At
back double doors open into a corridor which leads to the ballroom.
At left centre are double doors to the front hall. A great, luxurious
sofa is at the left, with chairs sociably near it, and on the other
side of the room a table has chairs grouped about it. On floral small
table are books and objets d'art, and everywhere there is a profusion
of white roses and maidenhair fern.

In the stage directions Left and Right mean Left and Right of actor,
as he faces audience.

Three smart-looking SERVANTS are peering through the crack of the
folding door, their backs to the audience. The pretty, slender MAID
is on a chair. The elderly BUTLER dignifiedly stands on the floor.
The plump, overfed little HOUSEMAID is kneeling so as to see beneath
the head of the BUTLER.

HOUSEMAID. [*Gasping.*] Oh, ain't it a beautiful sight!

BUTLER. [*Pompously.*] Not to me who 'ave seen a Lord married in Hengland.

MAGGIE. Oh, you make me sick, Mr. Potts, always talking of your English Aristocracy! I'm sure there never was no prettier wedding than this. Nor as pretty a bride as Miss Jinny.

BUTLER. [*Correcting her.*] Mrs. Haustin!

HOUSEMAID. She looks for all the world like one of them frosted angels on a Christmas card. My, I wish I could 'a' seen her go up the aisle with the organ going for all it was worth!

MAGGIE. It was a *beautiful* sight!

BUTLER. A good many 'appens to be 'aving the sense to be going now.

HOUSEMAID. Could you hear Miss Jinny say "I do," and make them other remarks?

MAGGIE. Yes, *plain*, though her voice was trembly like. But Mr. Austin he almost shouted!

[*Laughing nervously in excitement.*

BUTLER. 'E's glad to get 'er!

MAGGIE. *And her him!*

HOUSEMAID. Yes, that's what I likes about it. Did any one cry?

MAGGIE. Mrs. Tillman. Lots of people are going now.

HOUSEMAID. What elegant clothes! Oh, gosh!

BUTLER. [*Superciliously.*] Mrs. Cullingham don't seem in no 'urry; she's a common lot!

MAGGIE. I don't care, she's rich and Miss Jinny likes her; she just throws money around to any poor person or church or hospital that wants it, or *don't*! So she can't be so *very common* neither, Mr. Potts!

HOUSEMAID. Say, I catch on to something! Young Mr. Tillman's sweet on that there tall bridesmaid.

MAGGIE. [*Sharply.*] Who?

BUTLER. Miss Chester. I've seen there was something goin' hon between them whenever she's dined or lunched 'ere.

MAGGIE. [*Angry.*] 'Tain't true!

BUTLER. I'll bet my month's wages.

MAGGIE. I don't believe you!

BUTLER. Why, what's it to *you*, please?

MAGGIE. [*Saving herself.*] Nothing--

HOUSEMAID. Well, I guess it's truth enough. That's the second time I've seen him squeeze her hand when no one wasn't lookin'.

MAGGIE. Here, change places with me! [*Getting down from her chair.*] If you was a gentleman, Mr. Potts, you'd have given me *your place*!

[*Witheringly.*

BUTLER. If I was a *gentleman*, miss, I wouldn't be here; *I'd* be on the other side of the door.

[*He moves the chairs away.*

MAGGIE. [*To Housemaid.*] Honest, you saw something between them?

HOUSEMAID. Who?

MAGGIE. Him and her? Mr. Geoffrey and Miss Chester--

HOUSEMAID. *Cheese it!* they're coming this way!

[*She and the MAID and the BUTLER vanish through the door Right.*

[GEOFFREY and RUTH enter through the double doors quickly at back. GEOFFREY is a young, good-looking man, but with a weak face. He is of course very smartly dressed. RUTH is a very serenely beautiful girl, rather noble in type, but unconscious and unpretending in manner. They close the doors quickly behind them.

GEOFFREY. We'll not be interrupted here, and I must have a few words with you before you go.

[He follows her to the sofa where she sits, and leans over it, with his arm about her shoulder.

RUTH. Oh, Geof,--Geof, why weren't we married like this?

GEOFFREY. It couldn't be helped, darling!

RUTH. It isn't the big wedding I miss, oh, no, it's only it seemed sweeter in a church. Why did we have to steal off to Brooklyn, to that poor, strange little preacher in his stuffy back parlour, and behave as if we were doing something of which we were ashamed?

GEOFFREY. You love me, I love you,--isn't that the chief thing, dearest?

RUTH. But how much longer must we keep it secret?

GEOFFREY. Till I can straighten my affairs out. I can't explain it all to you; there are terrible debts,--one more than all the others,--a debt I made when I was in college.

RUTH. If I could only help you! I have a *little* money.

GEOFFREY. No, I love you too much; besides, this debt isn't *money*, and I hope to get rid of it somehow before long.

RUTH. Forgive me for worrying you. It is only that every one is so happy at this wedding except me,--dear Jinny brimming over with joy, as I would be,--and it's made me feel--a little--

GEOFFREY. [*Comes around the sofa and sits beside her.*] I know, dear, and it's made me feel what a brute I am! Oh, if you knew how I hate myself for all I've done, and for the pain and trouble I cause you now!

  [MAGGIE, her sharp features set tense, appears in the doorway on the left behind the curtains and listens.

RUTH. Never mind, we won't think of that any more.

GEOFFREY. I can never throw it off, not for a minute! I'm a worthless fellow and how can you love me--

RUTH. [*Interrupting him.*] I *do*! You are worth everything to me, and you will be worth much to the world yet!

GEOFFREY. I love you, Ruth--that's the one claim I can make to deserve you. But it's helped me to give up *all* the beastly pleasures I used to indulge in!

RUTH. [*Softly.*] Geof!

GEOFFREY. Which I used to think the only things worth living for, and which now, thanks to you, I loathe,--every one of them.

RUTH. I'm so glad! I've been some help, then.

GEOFFREY. If I'd only got you earlier, I'd have been a different man, Ruth!

RUTH. [*Smiling and taking his nervous hand in hers.*] Then I mightn't have fallen in love with you if you were a *different* man!

GEOFFREY. Dear girl! Anyway, this is the good news that I want to tell you--I hope now to have things settled in a couple of weeks.

RUTH. [*In glad relief.*] Geoffrey!

GEOFFREY. But--I mayn't be successful; it might be, Ruth--it might be, we would have to wait--for years--

RUTH. [*Quietly.*] I don't think I could bear that! It's not easy for me to lie and deceive as I've had to the last few months; I don't think I could keep it up.

[PETER CULLINGHAM enters suddenly, from the ballroom, a pale young man, but, unlike GEOFFREY, hard and virile.

PETER. Oh, here you are! I say, are you two spoony? Just the way *I* feel! [*Laughing.*] I caught and hugged old Mrs. Parmby just now! I think it's sort of in the air at weddings, don't you?

GEOFFREY. [*Rising.*] I'm surprised to see you've left the refreshment table, Peter.

PETER. They sent me to find Miss Chester--they're going to cut the bridesmaid's cake, and if you two really are spoony, Miss Chester, you'd better not miss it--you might get the ring!

[They laugh as PETER takes out a bottle from which he takes a round, black tablet which he puts in his mouth.

RUTH. [*Also rising.*] I'd better go.

[*PETER is making frantic efforts to swallow the tablet.*

GEOFFREY. [*Noticing him.*] What's the matter with you?

PETER. O dear! I've eaten so many ices and fancy cakes, I've got awful indigestion, and I'm trying to swallow a charcoal tablet.

RUTH. Come with me and get a glass of water.

PETER. No, it's very bad to drink water with your meals; but I'll get a piece of bridesmaid's cake--that'll push it down!

[*PETER and RUTH go out through the double doors.*

[The moment they are out of the room, MAGGIE comes from behind the curtain and goes straight up to GEOFFREY. He looks astonished and frightened.

GEOFFREY. What do you want? Have you been listening?

MAGGIE. So that's it, is it? You want to marry her when you can get rid of me.

GEOFFREY. [*With relief.*] What do you mean?

MAGGIE. Oh, I may not have heard everything, but I heard and saw enough to catch on that you're in love with Miss Chester.

GEOFFREY. Well?

MAGGIE. Well, you won't marry her--I'll never set you free.

GEOFFREY. Sh!

[*Looking about and closing the doors.*

MAGGIE. Oh, they're all in the dining room.

GEOFFREY. [*Angry.*] What do you want, anyway?

MAGGIE. [*She pleads a little.*] When I came here to your house and got a position, it was because I *loved* you, if you *had* treated me bad, and I hoped by seeing you again, and being near you, you might come back to me and everything be made straight!

GEOFFREY. Never! Never! It's impossible.

MAGGIE. [*Angry again.*] Oh, is it! Well, the dirty little money you
give me now only holds my tongue quiet so long's you behave yourself and
don't run after any other girls! But the minute you try to throw me
down, I'll come out with the whole story.

GEOFFREY. I was drunk when I married you!

MAGGIE. More shame to you!

GEOFFREY. You're right. But I was only twenty--and you--led me on--

MAGGIE. [*Interrupting him.*] Me! led you on! *me*, as decent and nice
a girl as there was in New Haven if I do do housework, and that's my
wedding ring and you put it there, and mother's got the certificate
locked up good and safe in her box with my dead baby sister's hair and
the silver plate off my father's coffin!

GEOFFREY. We mustn't talk here any more!

MAGGIE. You look out! If I wasn't so fond of your sister Miss Jinny,
and if the old people weren't so good to me, I'd just show you right
up *here--now*!

GEOFFREY. I'll *buy* you off if I can't divorce you!

MAGGIE. *You!* Poof!

[*GIRLS' voices are heard from the ballroom.*

GEOFFREY. Look out--some one's coming!

MAGGIE. [*Going.*] You haven't got a red cent; my cheque's always one of
your *father's*!

[*She goes out Right.*

GEOFFREY. Good God! what am I going to do--shoot myself, if I don't get out of this soon--I must get some air!

[*He goes out Left.*

[JINNY opens the double doors, looks in, and then enters. She is an adorable little human being, pretty, high-strung, temperamental, full of certain feminine fascination that defies analysis, which is partly due to the few faults she possesses. She is, of course, dressed in the conventional wedding-dress, a tulle veil thrown over her face.

JINNY. Not a soul! Come on!

[She is followed in by the four BRIDESMAIDS--nice girls every one of them--and also, very slyly, by SUSIE, a very modern spoiled child, who sits unobserved out of the way at the back.

Now, my dears, I wish to say good-by all by ourselves so I can make you a little speech! [*All laugh gently.*] In the first place I want to tell you that there's nothing like marriage! And you must every one of you try it! Really, I was never so happy in my life!

GRACE. Must we stand, or may we sit down?

JINNY. Oh, stand; it won't be long and you'll only crush your lovely frocks. In fact, I advise you not to lose any time sitting down again until you've got the happy day fixed!

RUTH. You know, Jinny darling, that there is no one so glad for your happiness as your four bridesmaids are--isn't that so, girls?

ALL. Yes!

[And they all together embrace JINNY, saying, "Dear old Jinny," "Darling Jinny," "We'll miss you dreadfully," etc., ad lib., till they get tearful.

JINNY. Good gracious, girls, we mustn't cry. I'll get red eyes, and Jack'll think what an awful difference just the marriage service makes in a woman.

[*The doors at the back open, and AUSTIN appears in the doorway.*

[AUSTIN is a typical New Yorker in appearance, thirty-two years old, good-looking, manly, self-poised, and somewhat phlegmatic in temperament.

AUSTIN. Hello! May a mere man come in to this delectable tea party?

JINNY. *No*, Jack! But *wait*--by the door till I call you!

AUSTIN. [*Amused.*] Thank you!

[*He goes out, closing the door.*

GERTRUDE. We'll miss you so awfully, Jinny.

JINNY. Just what I say! Get a man to keep you company, and then you won't miss any one.

BELLE. Yes, but attractive men with lots of money don't come into the Grand Central Station by every train!

JINNY. [*Putting her arm about her.*] You want too much, my dear Belle!

And you aren't watching the Grand Central Station either half so much as you are the steamer docks for a suitable person. Now don't be angry; you know you want a good big title, and you've got the money to pay, but, my dear Belle, it's those ideas of yours that have kept you single till--twenty-six!--now *that* you must confess was nice of me, to take off *three* years!

BELLE. [*Laughing.*] Jinny, you're horrid!

JINNY. No, I'm not! You know I'm *really* fond of you, or you wouldn't be my bridesmaid to-day; it's only that I want *your wedding* to be as happy as *mine*--that's all, and here's a little gift for you to remember your disagreeable but loving friend by!

[*Giving her a small jewelry box.*

BELLE. Thank you, Jinny! Thank you!

[*A little moved.*

GRACE. Mercy! I hope you're not going to take each one of us!

JINNY. I am, and come here, *you're* next!

GRACE. I'll swear I don't want to get married at all!

JINNY. Don't be silly, you *icicle*! Of course you don't; you freeze all the men away, so that you've no idea how nice and comfy they can be! My advice to you, Grace darling,--and I *love* you, or I wouldn't bother,--is to *thaw*! [*Laughs.*] I used to be awfully jealous of you--

GRACE. [*Interrupting.*] Oh!

JINNY. Yes, I was! You're lots prettier than I am.

GRACE. Jinny!

JINNY. You *are*! But I got over it because I soon saw you were so cold, there was no danger of any conflagration near you! Oh, I've watched your *eyes* often to see if any man had lighted the fires in them yet. And now I'm determined they shall be lighted. You're too *cold*! Thaw, dear,--not to *everybody*,--that would be like slushy weather, but don't keep yourself so continually so far below zero that you won't have time to strike--well--say eighty-five in *the shade*, when the right bit of masculine sunshine *does* come along! Here--with my best love!

[*Giving her a small jewelry box.*

[*GRACE kisses JINNY.*

GERTRUDE. I am the next *victim*, I believe!

JINNY. All I've got to say to *you*, Miss, is, that if you don't decide pretty soon on *one* of the half dozen men you are flirting with *disgracefully* at present, they'll every one find you out and you'll have to go in for widowers.

GERTRUDE. [*Mockingly.*] Horrors!

JINNY. Oh, I don't know! I suppose a widower is sort of *broken in* and would be more likely to put up with your caprices! For the sake of your charm and wit and true heart underneath it all, you dear old girl you!

[*Giving her a small jewel box.*

GERTRUDE. Thank you, Jinny. I'm only afraid I will do the wrong thing with you away! You know you're always my ballast!

JINNY. Nonsense! Female ballast is no good; masculine ballast is the only kind that's safe if you want to make life's journey in a love balloon. [*SHE turns to RUTH CHESTER.*] Ruth--the trouble with you is, you're too sad lately, and show such a lack of interest. I should think you might be in love, only I haven't been able to find the man. Anyway, if you aren't in love, you must *pretend* an interest in things. Of course, men's affairs are awfully dull, but they don't like you to talk about them, so it's really very easy. All you have to do is listen, stare them straight in the eyes, think of whatever you like, and look pleased! It *does* flatter them, and they think *they* are *interesting*, and you *charming*! Wear this, and think of me! [Giving her a box.] and be happy! I *want* you to be *happy*--and I can see you aren't!

RUTH. [*Kissing her.*] Thank you, dear!

JINNY. There, that's all!--except--when I come home from abroad in October, if every one of you aren't engaged to be married, I'll wash my hands of you--

[*They all laugh.*

[*SUSIE, sliding off her chair at back, comes forward.*

SUSIE. Now, it's my turn! You can't chuck me!

JINNY. [*Trying not to laugh.*] Susie! where did you come from and what do you mean?

SUSIE. Oh, you give me a pain!--I went up the aisle with you to-day, too--what's the matter with telling me how to get married!

JINNY. I'll tell you this, your language is dreadful; where do you get all the boy's slang? You don't talk like a lady.

SUSIE. I'm not a lady. I'm a little girl!

JINNY. You *talk* much more like a common boy.

SUSIE. Well, I'd rather *be* a *boy*!

JINNY. Susie, I shall tell Aunt Laura her daughter needs looking after.

SUSIE. Oh, very well, cousin Jinny. If you're going to make trouble, why, forget it!

  [*Turns and goes out haughtily, Right.*

JINNY. [*Going to the double doors, calls.*] Now you can come in, Jack.

  [*AUSTIN enters.*

AUSTIN. And now I've only time to say good-by. All your guests have gone except the Cullinghams, who are upstairs with your mother, looking at the presents.

GERTRUDE. Come! All hands around him!

  [*The five GIRLS join hands, with AUSTIN in the centre.*

BELLE. We don't care if every one else has gone or not, *we're* here yet!

AUSTIN. So I see! But I am ordered by my father-in-law--ahem! [all laugh] --to go to my room, or he thinks there will be danger of our losing our train.

ALL THE BRIDESMAIDS. [*Ad lib.*] Where are you going? Where are you going? We won't let you out till you tell us.

AUSTIN. I daren't--I'm afraid of my wife!

JINNY. Bravo, Jack!

GRACE. Very well, then, we'll let you out, on *one* condition, that you kiss us all in turn.

 [*The GIRLS laugh.*

JINNY. No! No! [*Breaking away.*] He shan't do any such thing!

 [*They all laugh and break up the ring.*

GERTRUDE. Dear me, isn't she jealous!

BELLE. Yes, it is evidently time we all went! Good-by, Jinny! [Kissing her.] A happy journey to *Washington*!

JINNY. No, it isn't!

 [General good-bys. JINNY begins with RUTH at one end, and AUSTIN at the other; he says good-by and shakes hands with each girl.

GERTRUDE. [*Kissing JINNY.*] Good-by, and a pleasant trip to Niagara Falls!

JINNY. Not a bit!

GRACE. [*Kissing JINNY.*] Good-by, I believe it's **Boston** or **Chicago**!

JINNY. *Neither!*

RUTH. Good-by, dear, and all the happiness in the world!

[*Kisses her.*

JINNY. Thank you.

[She turns and goes with the other three girls to the double doors at back, where they are heard talking.

RUTH. Mr. Austin?

AUSTIN. Yes?

[*Joining her.*

RUTH. [*Embarrassed.*] You like your new brother, **don't** you?

AUSTIN. Geof? most certainly I do, and Jinny adores him.

RUTH. I know, then, you'll be a good friend to him if he needs one.

AUSTIN. Surely I will.

RUTH. I think he does need one.

AUSTIN. Really--

[*The GIRLS are passing out through the doors.*

BELLE. Come along, Ruth.

[THEY pass out and JINNY stands in the doorway talking to them till they are out of hearing.

RUTH. Sh! please don't tell any one, not even Jinny, what I've said! I may be betraying something I've no right to do, and don't tell **him** I've spoken to you.

AUSTIN. All right!

[*JINNY turns around in the doorway.*

RUTH. Thank you--and good-by.

[*Shaking his hand again.*

[JINNY notices that they shake hands twice. A queer little look comes into her face.

AUSTIN. Good-by.

RUTH. Have they gone?--Oh! [*Hurrying past* JINNY.] Good-by, dear.

[*She goes out through the double doors.*

JINNY. [*In a curious little voice.*] Good-by....

[She comes slowly down the room toward AUSTIN, and smiles at him quizzically.] What were you two saying?

AUSTIN. Good-by!

JINNY. But you'd said it once to her already! Why did you have to say good-by *twice* to *Ruth*? Once was enough for all the other girls!

AUSTIN. [*Banteringly.*] The first time *I* said good-by to *her*, and the second time *she* said good-by to *me*!

JINNY. Do you know what I believe--*Ruth Chester's in love with you*!

AUSTIN. Oh, darling!

[*Laughs.*

JINNY. Yes, that explains the whole thing. No wonder she was *triste* to-day.

AUSTIN. [*Laughing.*] Jinny, sweetheart, don't get such an absurd notion into your head.

JINNY. [*Looks straight at him a moment, then speaks tenderly.*] No--no--I know it's not your fault. There was no other woman in this house for you to-day but *me*, *was* there?

AUSTIN. There was no other woman in the world for me since the first week I knew you.

[*Taking her into his arms.*

JINNY. This is good-by to *Jinny Tillman*!

[*He kisses her.*

Jack, darling, do you think I could sit on your knee like a little child
and put my arm around your neck and rest my head on your shoulder for
just five seconds--I'm *so tired*!

[*MRS. CULLINGHAM opens the door.*

MRS. CULLINGHAM. Oh!

[*Shuts the door very quickly and knocks.*

[*JINNY and AUSTIN laugh.*

JINNY. Yes, yes--come in!

[MRS. CULLINGHAM enters. She is a handsome, whole-souled, florid
woman; one of those creatures of inexhaustible vitality who make
people of a nervous temperament tired almost on contact by sheer
contrast. She is the kindest, best meaning creature in the world.

MRS. CULLINGHAM. Oh, do excuse me! I haven't any more tact!--and I hate
to interrupt you, but I must say good-by. [*Calls.*] Peter!

PETER. Yes'm.

[Entering with a glass of water and a powder. He sits in the
arm-chair at right, and constantly looks at his watch.

AUSTIN. I'm much obliged to you, Mrs. Cullingham, for the interruption,
as I was sent long ago to make myself ready for the train, if you'll
excuse me!

MRS. CULLINGHAM. Certainly!

JINNY. Good-by!

[*Taking his hand as he passes her.*

AUSTIN. Good-by!

[*He goes out Right.*

MRS. CULLINGHAM. If it's time for *him*, it's certainly time for *you*. I won't keep you a minute!

JINNY. No, really we've plenty of time,-- [*both sit on sofa.*] Wasn't it a lovely wedding!

MRS. CULLINGHAM. I never saw a sweeter, my dear! And it was perfectly elegant! Simply great!

JINNY. And isn't Jack--

MRS. CULLINGHAM. He is! And so are you! In fact I've been telling your mother I don't know how to thank you both. You've asked me to-day to meet the swellest crowd I've ever been in where I was *invited*, and didn't have to buy tickets, and felt I had a right to say something besides "excuse me," and "I beg your pardon." Of course, I've sat next to them all before in restaurants and at concerts, but this time I felt like the real thing myself, and I shall never forget it! If you or your husband ever want any mining tips, come to me; what my husband don't know about mines isn't worth knowing!

JINNY. I'm as glad as I can be if you've had a good time, and you mustn't feel indebted to us. Ever since we met in Egypt that winter, mamma and I have always felt you were one of our best friends.

MRS. CULLINGHAM. Of course you know it isn't for *my own* sake I'm doing these stunts to get into Society. It's all for *my boy*. He's *got* to have the best--or the *worst*, however you look at it! [*Laughing.*] Anyway, I want him to have a chance at it, and it belongs to him through his father, for my first husband was a real swell!

[*Looking at PETER lovingly.*

[At this moment, PETER, having again looked at his watch, tips up the powder on his tongue, and swallows it down with the water.

MRS. CULLINGHAM. Poor darling! He suffers terribly from indigestion. That's an alkali powder he takes twenty minutes after eating. Peter, we must say good-by now.

PETER. [*Coming up.*] Good-by, Miss Jinny.

MRS. CULLINGHAM. *Mrs. Austin!*

JINNY. Oh, I'll always be "Miss Jinny" to Peter!

PETER. Thank you! We've had a great time at your wedding! *Bully food!* But I'm *feeling* it! [*He turns aside.*] Excuse me!

MRS. CULLINGHAM. I was just telling Mrs. Austin--

[*Interrupted.*

JINNY. "Jinny"--don't change.

MRS. CULLINGHAM. Thank you-- [*Rises to go.*] I was just saying we won't forget in our social life, will we, Peter, that Miss Jinny gave us the biggest boost up we've had yet?

[*JINNY also rises.*

PETER. Well, you know, mother, I don't think the game's worth the candle. It's begun to pall on me already.

MRS. CULLINGHAM. I really think he's going to be superior to it!

PETER. I only go now for your sake.

[*MRS. TILLMAN, coming from Right, speaks off stage.*

MRS. TILLMAN. Jinny! Jinny!

JINNY. Mother!

[*MRS. TILLMAN enters.*

JINNY. I ought to dress?

MRS. TILLMAN. [*To MRS. CULLINGHAM.*] She'll be late if she isn't careful.

JINNY. I'm going to. Is Maggie there?

MRS. TILLMAN. Yes, waiting!

JINNY. Good-by. [*Kisses MRS. CULLINGHAM.*] Good-by. [Shakes PETER'S hand.]

PETER. Many happy returns!

[*JINNY goes out Right.*

MRS. TILLMAN. Come, I want to give you some of Jinny's flowers to take home with you. Would you like some?

MRS. CULLINGHAM. I should love them!

[*They go out through the doors at back.*

[PETER is suffering with indigestion. He takes a charcoal tablet, and SUSIE cautiously enters Right.

SUSIE. There you are! Have you got 'em?

PETER. No, I gave them back to you.

SUSIE. Then they're in there on the table--get 'em quick, the trunks are coming down now!

[PETER goes out quickly at back, as the BUTLER and MAN SERVANT enter Right, carrying a large new trunk with a portmanteau on top of it.

SUSIE. Put them right over there for a minute! [They put them down in the centre of the room, and the FOOTMAN goes out Right.] And mind, you don't split on us, Thomas. Auntie Tillman knows all about it--it's just to be a nice little surprise for Cousin Jinny and my new uncle.

BUTLER. Very well, miss.

[*He also goes out Right.*

[At the same time PETER reenters at back with a roll of papers and some broad white satin ribbon. The papers are about half a foot broad and two feet long, and on them is printed, "We are on our honeymoon."

PETER. [*With gay excitement.*] I've got 'em.

SUSIE. Get some water--there's sticky stuff on the back!

 [*PETER gives her the papers and ribbons and goes out again at back.*

SUSIE. Quick! [Ties a big white bow on the portmanteau and on a trunk handle.] If Auntie Tillman sees 'em, I'll bet she'll grab 'em off. She'll be as mad as *hops*!

 [The BUTLER and FOOTMAN reenter Right, and bring down an old steamer trunk and a gentleman's dressing-bag.

BUTLER. [*To the FOOTMAN.*] Go and see if the carriage is there!

FOOTMAN. Yes, sir.

 [*He goes out Left.*

 [*As PETER reenters from the back, with the water.*

SUSIE. Quick now! Quick!

 [*They stick one label on the big steamer trunk facing the audience.*

PETER. I say isn't that great!

 [SUSIE giggles aloud with delight. The BUTLER, standing at one side, smiles. They put another label on the other trunk.

SUSIE. [*Giggling.*] I heard them plan it,--they're taking one old trunk purposely so as people would not catch on they were just married!

[*Giggles delightedly.*

[*The FOOTMAN reenters with a driver, Left.*

FOOTMAN. Yes, sir, it's here.

BUTLER. [*To the driver.*] You can take that first.

[*Pointing to the steamer trunk.*

[*DRIVER goes out Left with it on his shoulder, and the portmanteau.*

BUTLER. Now, James, you're to go over with the luggage to Twenty-third Street Ferry and check the heavy baggage; you know where to.

FOOTMAN. Yes, sir.

SUSIE. [*Eagerly.*] Oh, *where to?*

BUTLER. I am hunder hoath not to tell, Miss.

SUSIE. O pish!

[Kneeling in the big arm-chair and watching proceedings from behind its back.

BUTLER. [*Continues to the FOOTMAN.*] And wait with the checks and Mr. Austin's dressing-bag-- [*Showing it.*] --until they come.

FOOTMAN. Yes, sir.

PETER. And make haste, or, I say, somebody'll turn up and give our whole joke away!

[*The DRIVER reenters.*

SUSIE. Yes, *do* hurry!

FOOTMAN. [*To the DRIVER.*] Come along.

[They take the big trunk out Left. BUTLER follows with the dressing-bag.

MRS. CULLINGHAM. [*Calls from the room at back.*] Peter darling, are you there?

SUSIE. Phew! Just in time!

[*Sliding down into a more correct position in the chair.*

PETER. Yes, mother!

[*Going to back.*

MRS. CULLINGHAM. [*In the doorway, at back.*] Come, take these beautiful roses from Mrs. Tillman!

[*MRS. CULLINGHAM and MRS. TILLMAN enter.*

MRS. TILLMAN. [*With her arms full of roses.*] Thomas will take them down.

PETER. No, I'd like to. Aren't they bully?

[*He takes them.*

MRS. CULLINGHAM. [*To MRS. TILLMAN.*] Good-by, and thank you again. I know you must want to go up to Jinny.

MRS. TILLMAN. Yes, she may need me to help her a little. Good-by. Good-by, Peter.

PETER. Good-by, ma'm.

[*MRS. TILLMAN goes out Right.*

MRS. CULLINGHAM. Why, Susie, how do you do?

SUSIE. [*Glides out of the chair and stands before it.*] How do you do?

[*Embarrassed.*

MRS. CULLINGHAM. You're a good little girl, I hope?

SUSIE. I don't! I hate good little girls!

MRS. CULLINGHAM. O my!

[*She goes out, laughing, Left.*

[PETER, coming to SUSIE, catches her in his arms and kisses her, much against her will.

SUSIE. [*Furious.*] Oh, you horrid, nasty thing, you! [She strikes at him; he runs; she chases him from one side of the room to the other, around a sofa and table, and out Left, screaming as she chases him.] I hate you! I hate you!

[*MAGGIE enters Right.*

MAGGIE. Miss Susie, Mrs. Tillman wants to see you upstairs.

SUSIE. What for?

MAGGIE. I don't know, Miss.

SUSIE. Pshaw! have I got to go? All right!

[*Going toward the door at Right.*

[*AUSTIN enters, meeting SUSIE.*

AUSTIN. Hello! Where are *you* going?

SUSIE. Oh, up to Auntie Tillman's room. Goodness knows what for; it's an awful bore! Want to come along?

AUSTIN. No, thank you; but if you see your Cousin Jinny, you might tell her I am down.

SUSIE. [*Hanging on to him.*] I say! Where are you and Cousin Jinny going to, anyway?

AUSTIN. [*Smiling.*] I don't know.

SUSIE. O my, what a fib! And that's a nice example to set a little girl!

[*She goes out Right.*

MAGGIE. [*Coming forward.*] I beg pardon, sir, but may I speak to you a minute?

AUSTIN. Certainly, Maggie, what is it?

MAGGIE. I've been trying for a chance to see you alone. I wouldn't bother you, sir--but it's only because I'm fond of Miss Jinny, and of Mr. and Mrs. Tillman, and they've all been so good to me; I know it would nearly kill 'em if they knew.

AUSTIN. Come, Maggie, knew what?

MAGGIE. Well, **one member** of this family ain't been good to me, sir. [From this point her feelings begin to get the better of her and she speaks rapidly and hysterically.] He's been bad, bad as he could, and somebody's got to talk to him, and I don't see who's a-goin' to do it but you. If he don't change, I'll not hold my tongue any longer. It's all I can do for their sakes to hold it now!

AUSTIN. Look here, what are you talking about? You don't mean Mr. Geoffrey?

MAGGIE. Yes, I do, sir; he's my husband.

AUSTIN. What!!

MAGGIE. We was married when he was at Yale, sir; I was in a shop there.

AUSTIN. But--! Well, after all, isn't this your and Geoffrey's affair? Why bring me in?

MAGGIE. Because he's making love to Miss Chester, and promising to marry **her** now, and if he don't stop--I'll make trouble!

AUSTIN. But if he's married to you, as you say--he can't marry--any one else.

MAGGIE. He's tried to make me believe our marriage ain't legal, because he was only twenty and he'd been drinking!

AUSTIN. What makes you think Mr. Geoffrey cares for--Miss Chester?

MAGGIE. I just heard and see him making love to her *here*!

AUSTIN. This is a pretty bad story, Maggie.

MAGGIE. Yes, sir, and the worst is, sir, I know I ain't good enough for him, and that's why I've kept still about it these three years, but I can't help loving him no matter how ugly he's treated me. [Breaking down into tears.] I just can't help it! I *love* him, sir, even if I'm only a servant girl, and I can't stand it thinking he's going to try and get rid of me for some one else!

   [*She sobs out loud.*

AUSTIN. Sh!--Maggie. Sit down a minute, and control yourself. Somebody'll hear you, and besides they'll be coming down presently. I'll have a talk with Mr. Geoffrey when I come back--

   [Interrupted as GEOFFREY enters Left. He doesn't see MAGGIE, who is collapsed in a corner of the sofa.

GEOFFREY. [*To AUSTIN.*] Ah! Thank goodness I've caught you; I had an awful headache and went out for a breath of air, and then I was afraid I might have missed you! I knew in that case Jinny would never forgive me, nor--I--myself--for that--matter--

[His voice grows less exuberant in the middle of his speech and finally at the end almost dies away, as he sees the expression in AUSTIN'S face and realizes that something is wrong somewhere. When he stops speaking, MAGGIE gives a gasping sob. He hears it, and starting, sees her.

GEOFFREY. Maggie!

AUSTIN. Geoffrey, is what this girl says true?

GEOFFREY. That I married her in New Haven? Yes.

MAGGIE. [*Rises.*] I'll go, please, I'd rather go.

AUSTIN. Yes, go, Maggie; it's better.

[*MAGGIE goes out Right.*

GEOFFREY. [*As soon as she is out of the room.*] Promise me, Jack, you won't tell any one! It's awful, I know! For two years at college I went all to pieces and led a rotten life,--and one night, drunk, I married her, and it isn't so much her fault. I suppose she thought I loved her,--but this would break up the old lady and gentleman so, if they knew, I couldn't stand it! And Jinny, for God's sake, don't tell Jinny. *She respects me.* You won't tell her, will you?

AUSTIN. No. But Maggie says you want to marry some one else now.

GEOFFREY. [*With a change, in great shame.*] That's true, too.

[*He sits in utter dejection on the sofa.*

AUSTIN. How are you going to do it?

GEOFFREY. I must make money somehow and buy off Maggie.

AUSTIN. Yes, go out to Sioux Falls, get a divorce there on respectable grounds, and settle a sum of money on Maggie.

GEOFFREY. But I can't do that!

AUSTIN. Why not?

GEOFFREY. I can't do anything that would give publicity, and that divorce would.

AUSTIN. Any divorce would; you can't get rid of that.

GEOFFREY. I tell you I can't have publicity. Ruth--Miss Chester--would hear of it.

AUSTIN. Well, if she loves you, she'll forgive your wild oats, especially as every one sees now what a steady, straight fellow you've become.

GEOFFREY. It's Ruth! But I can't do that. No, Jack, you must help--you will, won't you? Oh, *do*, for Jinny's sake! Help me to persuade Maggie to keep silent for good, tear up that certificate of marriage. I was only twenty; it's hardly legal, and I'll settle a good sum--

[*Interrupted.*

AUSTIN. [Going straight to him, puts his hand heavily on his shoulder.] Good God, you're proposing bigamy! You've done enough; don't stoop to *crime*!

[*The two MEN face each other a moment. GEOFFREY'S head drops.*

AUSTIN. Forget you ever said that; do what I tell you when Jinny and I have gone abroad, so she will be away from it a little, and if you want money, let me know.

[JINNY enters Right, with nervous gaiety, covering an upheaving emotion which is very near the surface.

JINNY. Ready! And there *you* are, Geof. I've been sending all over the house after you! Good-by! [*Throwing her arms about him.*] Dear old Geof! Haven't we had good times together! Always, always from the youngest days I can remember--I don't believe there were ever a brother and sister so sympathetic; I know there was never a brother such a perfect darling as you were--I'll miss you, Geof! [The tears come into her voice, anyway.] I used to think I'd never marry at all if I couldn't marry *you*, and I *do* think *he* is the only man in the world who could have taken me away from home, so long as you were there! [To AUSTIN, smiling.] You aren't jealous?

AUSTIN. No!

JINNY. [*In jest.*] Isn't it awful! You can't *make* him jealous! I think it's a positive flaw in his character! Not like--*us*, is he?

GEOFFREY. Dear old girl--

JINNY. [*Whispers to him.*] And I've noticed how you've overcome certain things, dear Geof. I know it's been *hard*, and I'm proud of you.

GEOFFREY. Sh! Jinny, dear old sister! I'll miss *you*! By George, Jin, the house'll be awful without--but you-- [*His voice grows husky.*] --just excuse me a minute!

[*He is about to break down, and so hurries out Right.*

JINNY. [*Sniffling.*] He was going to cry! Oh, Jack, you'll be a brother to Geoffrey, won't you? You know he's been awfully dissipated, and he's changed it all, all by himself! *If he should go wrong again*--I believe it would break my heart, I love him so!

AUSTIN. I'll do *more* for him, if he ever needs me, than if he were my own *brother, because he's* yours!

JINNY. [*Presses his hand and looks up at him lovingly and gratefully.*] Thank you. Wait here just a minute; I know he won't come back to say good-by. He's gone up to his room, I'm sure--I'll just surprise him with a hug and my hands over his eyes like we used to do years ago.

[She starts to go out Right, and meets MR. and MRS. TILLMAN, who enter.

TILLMAN. The carriage is here!

JINNY. I won't be a second--

[*She goes out Right.*

MRS. TILLMAN. Where has she gone?

AUSTIN. Up to her brother.

MRS. TILLMAN. Her father's been locked up in his study for three hours--he *says* thinking, but to *me* his eyes look very suspicious!

[*Taking her husband's arm affectionately.*

TILLMAN. [*Clears his throat.*] Nonsense!

MRS. TILLMAN. Well, *how many cigars did you smoke*?

TILLMAN. Eight.

MRS. TILLMAN. The amount of emotion that a man can soak out of himself with tobacco is wonderful! He uses it just like a sponge!

TILLMAN. Jack, the first thing I asked about you when I heard that--er--that things were getting this way was, does he smoke? A man who smokes has always that outlet. If things go wrong--go out and smoke a cigar, and when the cigar's *finished*, ten to one everything's got right, somehow! If you lose your temper, don't speak!--a cigar, and when it's finished, then speak! You'll find the temper all gone up in the smoke! A woman's happiness is safest with a man who smokes. [He clears his throat, which is filling.] God bless you, Jack, it *is* a wrench; our only girl, you know. She's been a great joy--ahem!

[*He quickly gets out a cigar.*

MRS. TILLMAN. [*Stopping him from smoking.*] No, no, dear, they're *going now*!

TILLMAN. Well, the best I can say is, I wish you as happy a married life as her mother and I have had.

MRS. TILLMAN. Thirty-five *dear* years! But now, George, let me say a word--you always have monopolized our new son--he'll be much fonder of you than *me*!

TILLMAN. Old lady!--Jealous!--

MRS. TILLMAN. Turn about is fair play--you're jealous still of Jinny and me. [*She pauses a moment.*] I think we'd better tell him!

TILLMAN. All right. The only rifts in our lute, Jack, have been little threads of jealousy that have snapped sometimes!

MRS. TILLMAN. Nothing ever serious--of course, **but** it's a fault that Jinny shares with us, and the **only fault** we've ever been able to find.

TILLMAN. We called her for years the girl with the green eyes. She goes it pretty **strong** sometimes!

AUSTIN. Oh, that's all right--I shall **like** it!

MRS. TILLMAN. You'll always bear with her, won't you, if she should ever get jealous of you?

AUSTIN. Of **me**? I'll never give **her the chance**.

MRS. TILLMAN. It isn't a question of chance; you just can't help it sometimes, can you, George?

TILLMAN. No, you can't.

MRS. TILLMAN. And so--

AUSTIN. Don't worry! Your daughter's safe with me. I'm not the jealous sort myself and I love Jinny so completely, so calmly, and yet with my heart, and soul, and mind, and body, she'll never have a **chance** even to **try** to be jealous of **me**!

TILLMAN. Sh!

[*JINNY enters Right.*

JINNY. I found poor Maggie up in my room crying! She says she can't bear to have me go away. I think she's sorry now she wouldn't come with me as maid--and I said good-by to cook and she sniffed!

[*AUSTIN looks at his watch.*

AUSTIN. Oh! we ought to go!

MRS. TILLMAN. Good-by, darling!

[Kissing JINNY and embracing her a long time, while AUSTIN and TILLMAN shake hands warmly and say good-by.

JINNY. [*Going to her father.*] Good-by, father. Dear old father!

[*With happy emotion.*

[*AUSTIN meanwhile is shaking hands with MRS. TILLMAN.*

JINNY. [*Returns to her mother.*] Darling--oh, how good you've always been to me! Oh, mummy darling, I *shall* miss you! You'll send me a letter to-morrow, won't you, or a telegram? Send a telegram--you've got the address!

MRS. TILLMAN. [*With tears in her eyes.*] Yes, it's written down!

JINNY. You can tell father, but no one else!

[*Hugs and kisses her mother.*

TILLMAN. Come, Susan! They'll lose their train!

[*JINNY again embraces her father.*

ALL. Good-by! Good-by!

[JINNY, starting to go with AUSTIN, suddenly leaves him and runs back again to her mother and throws herself in her arms. They embrace, in tears.

JINNY. Good-by, mother!

MRS. TILLMAN. Good-by, my darling!

TILLMAN. Come, come! they'll lose their train!

[JINNY runs to AUSTIN, and with his arms about her, they hurry to the door Left. They go through the doors at back to window in the corridor. JINNY stops at the door and she and AUSTIN face each other a moment.

JINNY. [*Looking up at him.*] Oh, Jack!

[She throws her arms about his neck and buries her face on his shoulder.

AUSTIN. Jinny, Jinny dear, you're not sorry?

JINNY. [Slowly raises her head and looks at him, smiling through her tears, and speaks in a voice full of tears and little sobs.] Sorry? Oh, no! Oh, no! It hurts me to leave them, but I never was so *happy* in my life!

[*He kisses her and they hurry out, with his arm about her.*

MRS. TILLMAN. [*In the corridor, lifts the window.*] I hear the door--

TILLMAN. There they are!

[SUSIE rushes across the stage with a bowl of rice in her arms and goes out Left.

[MR. and MRS. TILLMAN wave and say "Good-by!" "Good-by!" "Good-by!" They close the window in silence. The sound is heard as the window frame reaches the bottom. They turn and come slowly forward, TILLMAN wiping his eyes and MRS. TILLMAN biting her lips to keep the tears back. They come into the front room and stop, and for a second they look around the empty room. TILLMAN puts his hand in his pocket and takes out his cigar case. MRS. TILLMAN, turning, sees him; she goes to him swiftly and touches his arm, looking up at him through her tears. He turns to her and slowly takes her in his arms and holds her there close and kisses her tenderly on the cheek.

[*SUSIE enters Left, with empty bowl, sobbing aloud, as*

THE CURTAIN FALLS

ACT II

*(**Two months later**)*

The Vatican, Rome; the Tribune of the Apollo Belvedere; a semicircular room with dark red walls; in the centre is the large statue of Apollo. There are doorways at Right and Left. There is a bench on the right side of the room. A single LADY TOURIST enters Right, takes a hasty glance, yawns, and looking down at her Baedeker, goes out Left. A PAPAL GUARD is seen passing outside in the court. A FRENCHMAN and his WIFE (with Baedekers) are seen approaching; they are heard talking volubly. They enter Left.

BOTH. Ah!--

[*They stand a moment in silent admiration.*

HE. [*Reading from Baedeker.*] Apollo Belvedere. [*He looks up.*] C'est superb!

SHE. [*Beaming with admiration.*] Magnifique! Voila un homme!

HE. *Quelle grace!*

SHE. *Quelle force!*

[Both talk at once in great admiration and intense excitement for a few moments. Then he suddenly drops into his ordinary tone and manner.

HE. Allons, allons nous!

SHE. [*In the same tone.*] Oui, j'ai faim!

[*They go out Right.*

[JINNY and AUSTIN enter Left, he looking over his shoulder. They stand a moment just inside the doorway.

JINNY. What are you looking back so much for, Jackie?

AUSTIN. I thought I saw some one I know.

JINNY. Who?

AUSTIN. I didn't know who; it just seemed to be a familiar back.

JINNY. [*Playfully.*] Oh, come! I think the present works of art and your loving wife are quite enough for you to look at without hunting around for familiar backs!

AUSTIN. And Baedeker! [*Reading from Baedeker about the Apollo.*] Apollo Belvedere, found at the end of the fifteenth century, probably in a Roman villa--

JINNY. Of course, Apollo!

AUSTIN. Great, isn't it?

JINNY. Stunning! [*She turns and looks at him, smiling quizzically.*] *Still*--but I suppose I'm prejudiced!

AUSTIN. [*Obtuse.*] Still what?

JINNY. You dear old stupid! You know, Jack, you're deeply and *fundamentally* clever and brilliant, but you're not quite-- *bright--not quick*!

[*Laughing.*

AUSTIN. Don't you think having *one* in the family quick as chain lightning is enough? What have I missed this time, Jinny? You don't mean you've found a family likeness in the statue over there? I don't want to be unappreciative, but it doesn't suggest your father to me in the least,--nor even Geoffrey.

JINNY. *Stupid!!* Of course it doesn't *suggest* anybody to me--I was only thinking I sympathized with Mrs. Perkins of Boston,--don't you know the old story about her?

AUSTIN. No, what was it?

JINNY. [*After a quick look around to see that they are alone.*] Well--Mrs. Perkins from Boston was personally conducted here once and shown this very statue, and she looked at it for a few moments, and then turned around and said, "Yes, it's all right, but give *me Perkins*!"

AUSTIN. Jinny!

[*Laughing.*

JINNY. Are you shocked? Come, I'm tired; let's sit down here and read my letters--there's one from Geof.

[They sit on the bench at Right, and JINNY takes out a letter from GEOFFREY.

AUSTIN. I'll read ahead in Baedeker and you tell me if there's any news. [*He opens the Baedeker and reads, and she opens and reads the letter.*] Where is Geof's letter from?

JINNY. New York, of course; where else would it be?

AUSTIN. I had an idea he was going away.

JINNY. Geof! Where?

AUSTIN. West, a good way somewhere.

JINNY. But *why* would he go West?

AUSTIN. Oh, he had some business, I believe; I remember thinking it was a good idea when he told me. It was the day we were married--I was waiting for you to come downstairs.

JINNY. I think it's very funny Geof never said anything about it to *me*.

AUSTIN. My dear, what time had *you*? You were *getting married*!!

JINNY. I *was*! Thank heaven! I'm *so happy*, Jack!

[*Snuggling up to him on the bench.*

AUSTIN. [*Steals a little, quick hug with his arm about her waist.*]
Bless you, darling, I don't think there was ever a man as happy as I am!

[They start apart quickly as a GERMAN COUPLE enter Right, with a YOUNG DAUGHTER, who is munching a cake, and hanging, a tired and unwilling victim, to her mother's hand.

WOMAN. Ach! schoen! sehr schoen!!

MAN. Groesses, nicht?

WOMAN. *Yah!*

[*They stand admiring.*

AUSTIN. By the way, when you answer your brother's letter, I wish you'd say I seemed surprised he was still in New York.

JINNY. [*Reading.*] Um--um--

MAN. [*Wiping his warm brow.*] *Wunderbaum!*

WOMAN. *Yah!!*

[*They go out Left, talking.*

JINNY. [*Looking up from her letter.*] Oh! what do you think?

AUSTIN. That you're the sweetest woman in the world.

JINNY. No, *darling*, I mean *who* do you think Geoffrey says is over here and in Italy?

AUSTIN. I haven't the most remote idea! So far as *I've* been able to observe there has been absolutely *no one* in Italy but *you and me.*

JINNY. If you keep on talking like that, I shall kiss you!

AUSTIN. What! before the tall, white gentleman? [*Motioning to Apollo.*] I am dumb.

JINNY. [*Very lovingly.*] Silly! Well!--Mrs. Cullingham and Peter are over here and have brought Ruth Chester!

AUSTIN. [*Speaking without thinking.*] Then it *was* her back.

JINNY. [*With the smallest sharpening of the look in her eye.*] When?

AUSTIN. That I saw just now.

JINNY. [*With the tiniest suggestion of a strain in her voice.*] You said you didn't know whom it reminded you of.

AUSTIN. Yes, I know, I didn't quite.

JINNY. But if you thought it was Ruth Chester, why not have said so?

AUSTIN. No reason, dear, I simply didn't think.

JINNY. Well-- [*Sententiously.*] --*next time--think!*

AUSTIN. What else does Geoffrey say?

JINNY. Oh, nothing. The heat for two days was frightful--already they miss me more than he can say--

[*Interrupted.*

AUSTIN. I'll bet.

JINNY. Father smoked nineteen cigars a day the first week I was gone.

AUSTIN. *I* haven't *had* to smoke *any*!

JINNY. Mercy! don't boast!--and he thinks they will all soon go to Long Island for the summer.

AUSTIN. Doesn't he say a word nor a hint at his going West?

JINNY. No, he says he may go to Newport for August, and that's all.

[*Putting away letter, and getting out others.*

AUSTIN. Going to read all those?

JINNY. If you don't mind, while I rest. *Do* you mind?

AUSTIN. Of course not, but I think while you're reading I'll just take a little turn and see if I can't come across the Cullinghams.

[*Rising.*

JINNY. [After the merest second's pause, and looking seriously at him.] Why don't you?

AUSTIN. I'll bring them here if I find them--

[*He goes out Right.*

[JINNY looks up where he went off and gazes, motionless, for a few moments. Then she throws off the mood and opens a letter.

[Two tired Americans enter Right, a girl and her mother, MRS. LOPP and CARRIE.

MRS. LOPP. What's this, Carrie?

CARRIE. [*Looking in her Baedeker.*] I don't know; I've sort of lost my place, somehow!

MRS. LOPP. Well, we must be in Room No. 3 or 4--ain't we?

CARRIE. [*Reads out.*] The big statue at the end of Room No. 3 is Diana the Huntress.

MRS. LOPP. This must be it, then,--Diana! Strong-looking woman, ain't she?

CARRIE. Yes, very nice. You know she was the goddess who wouldn't let the men see her bathe.

MRS. LOPP. Mercy, Carrie! and did all the other goddesses? I don't think much of their habits. I suppose this is the same person those Italians sell on the streets at home, and call the Bather.

[*JINNY is secretly very much amused, finally she speaks.*

JINNY. Excuse me, but you are in one of the cabinets--and this is the Apollo Belvedere.

MRS. LOPP. Oh, thank you very much. I guess we've got mixed up with the rooms,--seems as if there's so many.

CARRIE. [*Triumphantly.*] There! I *thought* it was a man all the time!

MRS. LOPP. Well, what with so many of the statues only being piecemeal, as it were, and so many of the men having kinder women's hair, I declare it seems as if I don't know the ladies from the gentlemen half the time.

CARRIE. Did the rest of us go through here?

JINNY. I beg your pardon?

CARRIE. Thirty-four people with a gassy guide? We got so tired hearing him talk that we jes' sneaked off by ourselves, and now we're a little scared about getting home; we belong to the Cook's Gentlemen and Ladies.

JINNY. Oh, no, the others haven't passed through here; probably they have gone to see the pictures; you'd better go back and keep asking the attendants the way to the pictures till you get there.

MRS. LOPP. [*With rather subdued voice.*] Thank you! We've come to do Europe and the Holy Land in five weeks for $400--but I don't know, seems as if I'm getting awful tired--after jes' sevin days.

CARRIE. [*Affectionately.*] Now, mommer, don't give up; it's because you haven't got over being seasick yet; that's all!

JINNY. [*Helplessly.*] Oh, yes, you'll find it much less tiring in a few days, I'm sure.

MRS. LOPP. Still Rome does seem a powerful way from *home*! How'll we ask for the pictures?

CARRIE. Why, mommer! "Tableaux!" "Tableaux!" I should think you'd 'a' learned that from our church entertainments! Good-by; thank you ever so much.

MRS. LOPP. You haven't lost *your party*, too, have you?

JINNY. [*Smiling.*] I hope not! He *promised* to come back!!

MRS. LOPP. Oh! pleased to have met you--Good-by!

[*They start off Left.*

JINNY. No, not that way--back the way you came.

MRS. LOPP. Oh, thank you!

[She drops her black silk bag; out of it drop crackers, an account book, a thimble, a thread-and-needle case, a bottle of pepsin tablets, etc. They all stoop to pick the collection up, JINNY helping.

JINNY. [*Handing.*] I'm sure you'll want these!

MRS. LOPP. Yes, indeed; don't you find them coupon meals very dissatisfactory?

CARRIE. Thank you ever so much again. Come on, mommer!

[*MRS. LOPP and CARRIE go out Left.*

[*JINNY looks at her watch and goes back to her letter.*

[*MRS. CULLINGHAM enters Left.*

MRS. CULLINGHAM. [*Screams.*] Jinny!

JINNY. [*Jumps up.*] Mrs. Cullingham! [*They embrace.*] Did Jack find you?

MRS. CULLINGHAM. No, we haven't seen him! Ruth and Peter are dawdling along, each on their own; I like to shoot through a gallery. There's no use spending so much time; when it's over you've mixed everything all up just the same!

JINNY. [*Laughing.*] Well, I've this minute read a letter from Geoffrey saying you were over here. And Jack, who thought he got a glimpse of you a little while ago, went straight off to try and find you.

MRS. CULLINGHAM. What fun it is to see you--and how *happy* you look!

JINNY. I couldn't *look* as happy as I *feel*!

MRS. CULLINGHAM. [*Glancing at the statue.*] Who's your friend? Nice gent, isn't he?

   [*Laughing.*

JINNY. Mr. Apollo! Would you like to meet him?

MRS. CULLINGHAM. [*Hesitates.*] Er--no--I don't think! You must draw the line somewhere! He wouldn't do a thing to Corbett, would he?

JINNY. Who was Corbett?

MRS. CULLINGHAM. He was a prize fighter, and *is*--but that's another story-- Do you mean to say you've never heard of him?

JINNY. Oh, the name sounds familiar. But this, you know, is Apollo.

MRS. CULLINGHAM. No, I don't know; was he a champion?

JINNY. No, he was a Greek god!

MRS. CULLINGHAM. Oh, was he? Well, I wouldn't have cared about being in the tailoring business in those days, would you? Let's sit down. [They sit on bench Right.] Of course you know we wouldn't accept a thing like that in Peoria, where I come from, as a gift! No, indeed! If the King of Italy sent it over to our Mayor, he'd return it C.O.D.

JINNY. Sounds like Boston and the Macmonnies Bacchante!

MRS. CULLINGHAM. Oh, my dear, *worse* than that! It reminds me of a man at home who kept an underclothing store in our principal street and had a plaster cast of this gent's brother, I should think, in his window to show a suit of Jaegers on,--you know, a "combination"! And our Town Committee of Thirteen for the moral improvement of Peoria made the man take it out of his window and hang the suit up empty!

JINNY. Poor man!

MRS. CULLINGHAM. You ought to see our Park!--you know we've got a perfectly beautiful park,--and all the *men* statues wear Prince Alberts, and stand like this-- [She poses with lifted arm at right angle to body.] --as if they were saying, "This way out" or "To the monkey cage and zoo."

JINNY. [*Laughing.*] But the women statues?

MRS. CULLINGHAM. My dear! They only have heads and hands; all the rest's just clumps of drapery--we only have "Americans" and "Libertys," anyway. They apply the Chinese emigration law to all Venuses and *sich ladies*!

[*They both laugh.*

JINNY. Where did you say Peter and Ruth were?

MRS. CULLINGHAM. Well, I left Peter--who isn't at all well; I hoped this trip would help his indigestion, but it seems to have made it worse!--I left him--er--in a room with a lot of **broken-up Venuses**--I thought it was all right; he was eating candy, and there wasn't a whole woman among 'em!

JINNY. [*Slight strain in her voice.*] How did you happen to bring over Ruth Chester?

MRS. CULLINGHAM. Well, you know I always liked her. She never snubbed me in her life--I don't think any one you've introduced me to has been quite so nice to Peter and me as Mrs. Chester and her daughter.

JINNY. O they *are* real people!

MRS. CULLINGHAM. Ruth is terribly depressed over something. She's thin as a rail and the family are worried. She says there's nothing worrying her, and the doctors can't find anything the matter with her,--so Mrs. Chester asked me if I wouldn't take her abroad. They thought the voyage and change might do her good, and I seem to have a more cheery influence over her than most people. So here we are! [As PETER enters Left, eating.] Here's Peter! How do you think the darling looks?

PETER. How do you do, Mrs. Austin?

JINNY. How do you do, Peter? [*They shake hands.*] I'm sorry to hear you are seedy, but you eat too many sweet things.

PETER. I'm not eating candy; it's soda mints! [Showing a small bottle.] I *am* bad to-day, mother.

MRS. CULLINGHAM. If you don't get better, we'll go to Carlsbad.

JINNY. How do you like Rome, Peter?

PETER. Oh, I don't know--too much Boston and not enough Chicago to make it a real lively town.

JINNY. [*Laughing.*] I think I'll go look for Jack and tell him you've turned up.

MRS. CULLINGHAM. Perhaps he's found Ruth.

JINNY. [*With a change in her voice.*] Yes, perhaps.

 [*She goes out Right.*

PETER. [*Going to the doorway Right, calls after her.*] Ruth's in a room on your left, with rows of men's heads on shelves, Emperors and things,--but gee, such a *job lot*!

 [*Comes back and looks up at the statue.*

MRS. CULLINGHAM. Isn't it beautiful, Peter?

PETER. No, it's *too big*!

MRS. CULLINGHAM. Still this one isn't broken!

PETER. That's a comfort! Yes, it has been mended, too! [*Examining.*] Oh, yes, it's only another of these second-hand statues. Say, you missed one whole one, the best I've seen yet! A Venus off in a fine little room, all mosaics and painted walls,--that's where I've been.

MRS. CULLINGHAM. Why, Peter Cullingham! *Alone?* What kind of a Venus?

PETER. Oh, beautiful! I forgot to take my medicine!

MRS. CULLINGHAM. Was she--er--*dressed*, darling?

PETER. We--you know--she *had* been, but she'd sort of pushed it a good way off!

MRS. CULLINGHAM. [*With a sigh.*] You know we *ought* to admire these things, Peter darling; that's partly what we've come to Europe for!

PETER. O pshaw! here comes a gang of tourists. Come on, let's skip!

MRS. CULLINGHAM. But Ruth and Mrs. Austin?

PETER. We didn't agree to wait, and we can all meet at our hotel.

[A crowd of TOURISTS, led by a GUIDE, presses and crowds in the doorway. They drag their tired feet in a listless shuffle across the room and stand in a somewhat sheepish and stupid bunch at the statue. One or two of the younger women nudge each other and giggle. The GUIDE stands a little in advance of them. The GUIDE describes the statue, and while he is doing so PETER and MRS. CULLINGHAM go out Right. Most of the TOURISTS turn and watch them go instead of looking at the statue.

GUIDE. This is the Apollo Belvedere, discovered at the end of the fifteenth century, some say in a Roman villa or farm-house near the Grotter Terratter. Very fine specimen both as marble and man. This statyer is calculated to make Sandow et cetery look like thirty cents.

Height seven feet, weight--

A MAN TOURIST. How much?

A GIRL TOURIST. Was he married?

[*Titters from the group.*

GUIDE. Give it up! Should judge he was. The god once held a bow in his left hand and probably a laurel wreath in his right.

ANOTHER WOMAN TOURIST. A what?

GUIDE. A laurel wreath. You want to take a good look at this, as it is a very fine piece. Now come along, please--make haste; we must finish up this place before feeding!

[He leads the way out Right, and the TOURISTS follow, shuffling along, without speaking, MRS. LOPP and CARRIE lagging in the rear.

[*AUSTIN enters Left, followed by RUTH.*

AUSTIN. This is where I left her with Apollo! [*Calls.*] Jinny! She seems to have gone!

[*He looks behind the statue and out door, Right.*

RUTH. Probably the Cullinghams, who were headed in this direction, found her, and they've all gone back for us; you see I walked all around the court first without going into the rooms, so I missed them, but found you.

AUSTIN. What shall we do? Sit down here and wait for them to come back, or shall I go in search?

RUTH. Oh, no, you might miss them, and then we'd all be lost! If you left Jinny here, she's sure to come back to meet you.

[*She sits on the bench and AUSTIN stands behind her.*

AUSTIN. I'm sorry to learn you've been ill.

RUTH. Oh! it's nothing.

AUSTIN. Ah, I'm afraid it's a good deal. Will you forgive me if I say I think I know what it is!

[*She looks up startled.*

[*After a moment.*

You haven't forgotten the day of Jinny's and my wedding, when you told me Geoffrey Tillman needed a friend?

RUTH. I hoped *you'd* forgotten; I oughtn't to have told you; I *oughtn't* to have!

AUSTIN. Why not? I had a talk with Geoffrey, then, and he told me everything.

RUTH. He did! You are sure?

AUSTIN. Sure.

[*He sits beside her.*

RUTH. That he and I--

AUSTIN. Love each other.

RUTH. Oh, but that isn't all.

AUSTIN. I know the rest!

RUTH. He told you--about--about--

AUSTIN. The marriage?--Yes?

RUTH. Oh, I'm so glad, so glad! Now I can speak of it to some one, and some one who can advise me, and will help us.

AUSTIN. I have already advised him, but he doesn't seem to be taking my advice; it has worried me.

RUTH. When I left he was awfully depressed. He said he saw no prospect of being able to publish our marriage for years, maybe!

AUSTIN. *What* marriage?

[*In astonishment.*

RUTH. *Our* marriage, in Brooklyn! [She notices his expression and is alarmed.] You said he had told you!

AUSTIN. [*Recovering himself, and speaking at first with hesitation.*] Yes, but not the details, not--wait, I'm a little confused. [Rising and walking a moment.] Let's get it all quite clear now, that's the only way I can help you--both; I ought, of course, to have gone through it all with him, but there really wasn't time.

RUTH. I can't go on like this much longer. It's killing me to deceive mother; I *must* tell her soon!

AUSTIN. [*Quickly, stops walking.*] No. You mustn't, not yet, if I'm going to help you; you'll obey me, won't you?

RUTH. Yes, if you only will help us!

AUSTIN. You said you and Geoffrey Tillman were married where?

RUTH. In Brooklyn.

AUSTIN. When?

RUTH. A month before your wedding.

AUSTIN. [*To himself.*] It's impossible!

[*Walking up and down.*

RUTH. [*Smiling sadly.*] Oh, no! I remember the date only too well.

AUSTIN. I didn't mean that.

RUTH. I lied to my mother that day for the first time--at any rate, since I was a child--and I've been lying to her ever since.

AUSTIN. [*Probing her.*] But--but why were you married so secretly?

RUTH. We couldn't afford to marry and set up for ourselves. He expected then to be sent off at once to the Philippines, and--well he didn't want to leave me behind, free; I'm afraid he's rather jealous--you must have found out by now that Jinny is. They all are! And *I* didn't want him to go so far off without my belonging to him either; *I'm* that jealous, too! [*Smiling.*] So--that's why!

AUSTIN. And this long period of secrecy since then--do you understand that?

Ruth. Hasn't he explained to you his debts? You know before he loved me he was very fast, but since--

AUSTIN. Yes, I know how he gave up every one of his old habits with a great deal of courage.

RUTH. *Nobody* knows what it cost him! How can you help us? Get him something to do to pay off his debts? Or can't you make him feel even if we do have to go on living at our different homes for a while, it is better to publish the fact that we are married?--

AUSTIN. I shall go back at once to America if I can persuade Jinny!

RUTH. And I, too?

AUSTIN. No. You must stay abroad till I send word for you to come home. If I am going to help you, you will help me by doing exactly as I say, won't you?

RUTH. Yes.

AUSTIN. It's *very* important that you should *absolutely obey me*!

RUTH. *I will.*

[*A pause.*

[JINNY, unnoticed by either of them, appears in the doorway at Right. AUSTIN is walking up and down. RUTH is leaning her elbow on the back of the bench and burying her face in her hands.

AUSTIN. It's awful! My God, it's awful!

JINNY. [*In a strained, assumed, nonchalant tone.*] *What is?*

RUTH. Jinny!

 [*Rising.*

AUSTIN. I didn't hear you, Jinny!

JINNY. No, you both seemed so absorbed.

RUTH. [*Going to JINNY.*] I'm so glad to see you.

 [Kisses her, but JINNY only gives her her cheek and that rather unwillingly; she is looking all the time at her husband.

JINNY. Thank you, I've just left the Cullinghams. They sent word to you they were going and would wait for you outside.

RUTH. Oh, then, I mustn't keep them waiting. We'll all meet at dinner to-night, won't we? Good-by--good-by.

 [*With a grateful look at AUSTIN, she goes out Right.*

JINNY. [*Watches her go; then turns to AUSTIN.*] That wasn't true, what I told her--I haven't seen the Cullinghams, and I don't know where they are, and what's more, I don't care!

AUSTIN. What do you mean?

JINNY. [*Beginning by degrees to lose control of herself.*] What did *she* mean by *following you* to Rome?

AUSTIN. Jinny!

JINNY. Oh, don't try to deny it; that'll only make me suspect *you*!

AUSTIN. My dear girl, you don't know what you're saying!

JINNY. She's ill, they say at home! Yes, and they don't know what's the matter with her, do they? No! But I can tell them! She's in love with another woman's husband!

AUSTIN. [*Taking her hand.*] Hush! I won't allow you to say such things!

JINNY. [*With a disagreeable little laugh.*] Oh, won't you? *You'd* better be careful,--my eyes are opened!

AUSTIN. Yes, and much too wide.

JINNY. A half-blind person would have known there was something between you two. When I came into this room just now, it was in the air--it was in both your faces!

[*She sits on the bench.*

AUSTIN. You've worked yourself up to such a pitch you're not responsible for what you're saying!

JINNY. *I* not *responsible*! What was it you were saying was *so* "awful" when I came in here? "My God, so awful!"

[*He doesn't answer.*

[*Almost hysterical, she rises.*

She had told you she loved you! She'd confessed she'd followed you over here!

AUSTIN. Absolutely false, **both** your suppositions!

JINNY. Oh, of course you'd protect her; you're a gentleman! But if I **thought** you **knew** she was coming over--

AUSTIN. Jinny! Jinny! How **can** you have such a thought?

JINNY. Well, why didn't you tell me when you thought you saw her a little while ago?

AUSTIN. Oh--

JINNY. Oh, it's very easy to say "Oh!" [*Imitating him.*] but why didn't you?

AUSTIN. I told you I didn't think who it was; I only thought something familiar flashed across my eyes. Jinny darling, this is sheer madness on your part, letting yourself go like this. It has no reason, it has no excuse! Ask your own heart, and your own mind, if in speaking to **me** as you have, you haven't done me at least an injustice and my love for you a **little** wrong.

JINNY. Well, I'm sure **she's** in love with you, anyway.

AUSTIN. No, she isn't! And it's disgraceful of you to say so! I know she isn't--

JINNY. How do you know she isn't?

AUSTIN. There's no question of it. I'm sure of it! You mustn't think, dear, that because *you* love me, everybody does--you idealize me!

[*Smiling apologetically.*

JINNY. Oh, you're so modest you don't see! but I do--on the steamer, in the hotels, everywhere we go, always, all the women admire you awfully! I see it!

AUSTIN. [*Laughing.*] What utter nonsense! [*Taking her into his arms.*] You've got something in your *eyes*!

JINNY. Only tears!

AUSTIN. No, something else,--something *green*.

JINNY. [*Laughs through her tears.*] Somebody's told you my old nickname!

AUSTIN. What?

JINNY. [*Laughs and is a little embarrassed.*] The girl with the green eyes.

AUSTIN. Ahem!--

JINNY. Well, I don't care if it is appropriate, I can't help it.

[*Slipping from his arms.*

AUSTIN. You must--or it will threaten our happiness if you let yourself be carried away by jealousy for no earthly reason outside of your dear, little imagination, like you have this time--

[*Interrupted.*

JINNY. You honestly don't think she cares for you?

AUSTIN. Not a bit!

JINNY. But what was it you were so serious about--what *is* between you?

AUSTIN. She is in a little trouble, and I happen to know about it.

JINNY. How?

AUSTIN. [*After a second's hesitation.*] That you mustn't ask me; it was not from her I knew of it.

JINNY. Truly?

AUSTIN. Truly.

JINNY. I don't care, she hadn't any business to go to you! I should think she'd have gone to a *woman* instead of a *man* for sympathy. She's got Mrs. Cullingham!

AUSTIN. She can't go to her, poor girl. Mrs. Cullingham knows nothing about it.

JINNY. Now don't you get too sympathetic--*that's very dangerous*!

AUSTIN. Look out, your imagination is peeping through the keyhole.

[*A moment's pause.*

JINNY. [*In a sympathetic tone, the jealousy gone.*] What is her trouble, Jack?

AUSTIN. That, dear, I can't tell you now; some day, perhaps, if you want me to, but not now. Only I give you my word of honor, it has nothing to do with you and me--does not touch our life! And I want you to tell me you believe me, and *trust* me, and won't let yourself be jealous again!

JINNY. I do believe you, and I do trust you, and I will *try* not to be jealous again!

AUSTIN. That's right.

JINNY. You know that book of De Maupassant's [They move away together.] I was reading in the train the other day,--about the young girl who killed herself with charcoal fumes when her lover deserted her?

AUSTIN. [*Half laughing.*] This is apropos of what, please? I have absolutely *no* sympathy with such people.

JINNY. In America that girl would have simply turned on the gas.

AUSTIN. You're getting morbid, Jinny!

JINNY. No, I'm not! but if ever--

AUSTIN. [*Interrupting--laughing it off.*] I shall install electric light as soon as we get home!

[*They both laugh.*

JINNY. I'm sorry I was so disagreeable to Ruth, but I'll try to make up for it in every way I can.

[*She sits on the bench and he leans over the back toward her.*

AUSTIN. There's one other thing, Jinny, I'd like to speak of now. Would you mind giving up the Lakes and going home this week?

JINNY. Going *home*--at once?

AUSTIN. Yes-- *Wall Street* is very uncertain. I'm worried,--I don't mind telling you,--and I want to see Geoffrey about his business.

JINNY. [*Half in earnest.*] Jack! You're not running away from *her*, are you?

AUSTIN. Jinny! *After all* we've said!

JINNY. No! I wasn't in earnest! I'm ready to go. I've seen the Lakes, and whether you are in Italy or in New York, so long as we are together, it's our honeymoon just the same.

AUSTIN. And may it last *all our lives*!

JINNY. Still, I don't mind owning up that leaving Ruth Chester behind here is rather pleasanter! [*She rises quickly with a sudden thought.*] *She* is not going back, too?

AUSTIN. Oh, no, not for a long time. They are over here indefinitely.

JINNY. I've been too horrid and nasty for words this morning, Jack--I'm so sorry.

AUSTIN. It's over and forgotten now.

JINNY. You *do* forgive me?

AUSTIN. Of course, dear; only I want to say this one thing to you: to suspect unjustly a *true* love is to insult that love!

JINNY. I didn't really suspect you.

AUSTIN. Of course I know you didn't; this is only by way of a grandfatherly warning! It is possible to insult a true love too often--and love can die--

JINNY. Sh! don't, please, say any more. You have forgiven me, haven't you?

AUSTIN. Yes!

JINNY. Then kiss me!

AUSTIN. [*Smiling.*] Here! My dear, some one will see us!

JINNY. No, only Apollo; see, there's no one else about--it's luncheon hour!

AUSTIN. But--

[*Taking her hand.*

JINNY. [*Pulling him.*] Come along, then, behind the statue. No one will see us there!

[They are behind the statue a moment and then come around the other side.

JINNY. There! no one saw us, and I'm so *happy*, are you?

AUSTIN. *"So happy!"*

[JINNY takes his arm and they go to the Left entrance. She stops and looks up at him.

JINNY. Are my eyes *green* now?

AUSTIN. Now they're *blue*!

JINNY. Hurrah! and I'm going, from now on, to be *so good*, you won't know me.

[*And hugging his arm tight they go out as*--

THE CURTAIN FALLS

ACT III

(Three weeks later)

The Austins' library; a warm, attractive room, with dark woodwork, and the walls hung in crimson brocade; Dutch marqueterie furniture; blue and white china on the mantel and tops of the book shelves; carbon photographs of pictures by Reynolds, Ronney, and Gainsborough on the wall. There is a double window at the back. A door at Right leads to the hall, and another on the Left side of the room leads to JINNY's own room. MRS. TILLMAN sits at a pianola Right, playing "Tell me, Pretty Maiden"; she stops once in a while, showing that she is unaccustomed to the instrument. JINNY enters from Left, singing as her mother plays.

JINNY. Darling mother!

[*She puts her arms about her and kisses her.*

[*They come away from the pianola together, to a big arm-chair.*

MRS. TILLMAN. I really must get one of those sewing-machine pianos for your father. I believe even he could play it, and it would be lots of amusement for us.

JINNY. Jack adores it; I gave it to him for an anniversary present.

MRS. TILLMAN. What anniversary?

[*Sitting in the chair.*

JINNY. Day before yesterday. The eleventh Tuesday since our marriage. Have you been in town all day? I *am* glad to see you!

[*She sits on the arm of the chair with her arm about her mother.*

MRS. TILLMAN. Yes, and I told your father to meet me here and we'd take the six-thirty train from Long Island City.

JINNY. Jack and I are going to the theatre to-night.

MRS. TILLMAN. I thought they were all closed!

JINNY. Oh, no, there are several musical comedies on,--Jack's favorite form of amusement,--and I've bought the tickets myself for a sort of birthday party.

MRS. TILLMAN. Is it his birthday?

JINNY. No, that's only my excuse!

MRS. TILLMAN. [*Laughing.*] Had we dreamed you and Jack were coming home in June, your father and I wouldn't have gone into the country so early.

JINNY. We've been home two weeks and it hasn't been hot yet.

MRS. TILLMAN. And you're still ideally happy aren't you, darling?

JINNY. Yes--

[She rises and goes to a table near the centre of the room and looks at the titles of several books without realizing what they are.

MRS. TILLMAN. Why, Jinny,--what does that mean?

JINNY. Oh, it's all my horrid disposition!

MRS. TILLMAN. Been seeing green?

JINNY. Um! Um! Once in Rome, and on the steamer, and again since we've been back.

MRS. TILLMAN. Nothing serious?

JINNY. [*Hesitatingly, she turns and faces her mother.*] No--but the last time Jack was harder to bring around than before, and he looked at me for fully five minutes without a particle of love in his eyes, and they were almost--*dead* eyes!

MRS. TILLMAN. What was it all about?

JINNY. Ruth Chester, principally.

MRS. TILLMAN. Why Ruth?

JINNY. Well, the first real scene I made was in Rome in the Vatican. I was jealous of her; I can't explain it all to you--as a matter of fact, it hasn't been all explained to *me*! Something was troubling Ruth that Jack knew, and he said he'd help her.

MRS. TILLMAN. What?

JINNY. That's just it; Jack won't tell me. And the day we sailed from

Naples a telegram came, and of course I opened it, and it said, "Trust me, I will do everything you say. Ruth."

MRS. TILLMAN. Why haven't you told me anything of all this before, dear?

JINNY. [*Going back to her mother.*] I was ashamed to! Somehow, in the end I always knew I was wrong and had hurt him--hurt him terribly, mother, the man I love better than everything else in the world! Yes, even better than you and father and Geoffrey--all together!

[*In her mother's arms, crying a little.*

MRS. TILLMAN. Oh, this curse of jealousy! I was in hopes he was so strong he would help you to overcome it.

JINNY. He does try hard, I can see sometimes; but he hasn't a spark of it in him, and he can't understand it, and I know I'm unreasonable, and before I know it I am saying things I don't know what, and some day he won't forgive them! I'm sure some day he won't!--

[*Breaking down again.*

[*She rises and turns away.*

MRS. TILLMAN. [*Rising and putting her arms about her.*] Come, dear! Now you're getting yourself all unstrung, and that won't do you any good; you've got to fight this battle out, I'm afraid, by yourself, trusting in the deep love of your husband to teach him forbearance. Your father's and my troubles were never very big because we *shared* the curse, so we knew how to sympathize with each other!

JINNY. What an awful thing it is!

MRS. TILLMAN. Yes, my dear child. Jealousy has no saving grace, and it only destroys what is always most precious to you. Jinny, don't let it destroy **your best** happiness!

JINNY. Mother, if it **should**, I'd kill myself!

MRS. TILLMAN. [**Shocked, but quite disbelieving her.**] My dear!

[**MAGGIE enters Right.**

MAGGIE. Mr. Tillman is downstairs, madam.

MRS. TILLMAN. Tell him to come up.

MAGGIE. Yes, madam.

[**She goes out Right.**

JINNY. Don't tell father anything before me.

MRS. TILLMAN. I don't know that I shall tell him at all; he would only advise more cigars!

[**TILLMAN enters Right.**

[**MRS. TILLMAN sits on the sofa at Left.**

TILLMAN. Are you here?

JINNY. [**Going to meet him.**] We are, father dear, and your presence **almost** completes us. [**Kisses him.**] I say **almost**, because Jack hasn't come up town yet, and Geoffrey's heartless enough to stay on fishing at Cape Cod!

TILLMAN. No, he isn't; he's back to-day.

[*He sits in the arm-chair at Right.*

JINNY. Oh, I do want to see him!

[*Sitting near her father.*

TILLMAN. He ought to have been in by now--I met them this morning. He was to lunch with Jack, and he's going to put up for a few days at the University.

JINNY. He must dine with us every night.

TILLMAN. Jinny!-- [*Looking at her.*] --You look as if you've been crying!

[*The two WOMEN are embarrassed, and JINNY doesn't reply.*

TILLMAN. [*Hurt.*] Oh, if you prefer to have secrets from your father, it's all right! *I don't begrudge* your mother her *first place* in your affections!

JINNY. Not at all, father; with you and mother there's no first place. She will tell you all about it on the way home! Please, mother.

MRS. TILLMAN. Very well, dear.

TILLMAN. A little "scrap" between you and Jack?

JINNY. Yes, but it's all over!

TILLMAN. Um!-- [Thinks a second, then taking out his cigar case, he empties it of cigars and hands them to JINNY.] Give your husband these, please, when he comes in!

[*JINNY and her MOTHER exchange a smile.*

JINNY. But, father, Jack's got boxes full--

TILLMAN. Never mind; give him those, *from me, with my compliments*!

JINNY. [*Laughing.*] Very well!

TILLMAN. How are you and Maggie getting on?

JINNY. Splendidly.

MRS. TILLMAN. Such a nice girl!

JINNY. And wasn't it odd Jack was bitterly opposed to my taking her?

MRS. TILLMAN. My dear, if we hadn't lent her to you for these few weeks, you wouldn't have got anybody decent for so short a time.

TILLMAN. Why didn't Jack want her to come?

JINNY. I don't know, he just didn't want her; and then last week he talked with her in the library for three-quarters of an hour by my watch.

MRS. TILLMAN. Why?

JINNY. Oh, it seems *she* has troubles, too! All single young women with troubles, of no matter what class, seem to make a bee line for my husband, even if they have to cross the ocean!

TILLMAN. What do you mean?

JINNY. [*Half laughing.*] Oh, nothing, but it was about that talk with Maggie that we had our last quarrel.

[*MAGGIE enters Right.*

MAGGIE. Mrs. Cullingham.

[*A second's dead silence, the announcement falling like a bombshell.*

JINNY. [*Astounded.*] *Who?*

[*She rises.*

TILLMAN AND MRS. TILLMAN. *Who?*

MAGGIE. Mrs. Cullingham and her son, madam.

JINNY. They're in Europe.

MRS. TILLMAN. Are you sure you're not mistaken, Maggie?

MAGGIE. Oh, yes'm. Even if you *could* mistake Mrs. Cullingham, you couldn't mistake Mr. Peter!

JINNY. Ask them to please come up, Maggie.

MAGGIE. Yes'm.

[*She goes out Right.*

TILLMAN. Why, they only just sailed the other day, didn't they?

MRS. TILLMAN. Yes, and they were supposed to be gone all summer at least, for Ruth Chester's health! What in the world can they have come back for?

JINNY. [*With curious determination.*] *That* is what *I* intend to find out.

TILLMAN. [*Rising.*] We must be going, Susan; we've lost our train as it is.

MRS. TILLMAN. [*Rising.*] We can take the seven-two.

[MAGGIE shows in MRS. CULLINGHAM and PETER. PETER shakes hands with MRS. TILLMAN, then with JINNY, and then with MR. TILLMAN.

[MRS. CULLINGHAM kisses MRS. TILLMAN and shakes hands with MR. TILLMAN.

MRS. CULLINGHAM. Jinny, you angel, aren't you surprised!

[*Kissing her.*

JINNY. Well, rather!

MRS. CULLINGHAM. Well, you aren't a bit more surprised than I am. [A clock strikes six-thirty.] There goes the half hour, Peter; you must take your powder.

PETER. I beg your pardon, mother; it's the tablet now.

MRS. CULLINGHAM. Excuse me, dear, I'm so dead tired.

[*Sits on the sofa.*

JINNY. [*To Peter.*] Will you have some water?

PETER. No, thank you, I've learned now to take them *au naturel*, and without much, if any, inconvenience!

[Takes his tablet with still a certain amount of difficulty, and sits Right.

MRS. TILLMAN. [*To MRS. CULLINGHAM.*] Did you have a bad voyage?

MRS. CULLINGHAM. No, perfectly beautiful!

PETER. [*Reproachfully, and with a final swallow.*] Oh, mother!

MRS. CULLINGHAM. Except, of course, for poor Peter; he gets worse every trip! He can eat *absolutely nothing*--that is *for long*! But it's the Custom House that's worn me out; I was there from twelve till four.

MRS. TILLMAN. But you wouldn't have had time to buy anything!

MRS. CULLINGHAM. Of course not! But I took plenty of new dresses for the entire summer; most of them hadn't been worn, and they were determined to make me pay duty.

JINNY. We had to pay awfully for things! I wanted to try and smuggle, but Jack wouldn't let me!

MR. TILLMAN. I'm afraid *we* must go!

[*ALL rise.*

MRS. CULLINGHAM. What do you think the Inspector had the impudence to ask me finally,--if I wanted to bring the dresses in as theatrical properties!

[*They laugh.*

MRS. TILLMAN. You must have some *gorgeous* frocks!

MRS. CULLINGHAM. Oh, there are some *paillettes*! But who do you suppose he took me for--Sarah Bernhardt!

TILLMAN. [*Looking at his watch.*] I don't wish to interrupt this vital political conversation, but, Susan, if you don't want to miss the seven-two train, too--!

MRS. TILLMAN. [*Rising.*] Oh, no, we mustn't do that. Good-by. [To MRS. CULLINGHAM, shaking hands.] It's nice to see you again, anyway. Is Ruth better?

MRS. CULLINGHAM. I'm sorry to say--I don't think she is--good-by.

[*To MR. TILLMAN, who says good-by--general good-bys.*

MRS. TILLMAN. [*To JINNY.*] You want me to tell your father?

JINNY. Yes, it's better; it does make him jealous if he thinks I tell you things and keep secrets from him.

TILLMAN. Good-by, Peter.

MRS. TILLMAN. Good-by, Peter.

PETER. By-by.

[MR. and MRS. TILLMAN quickly go out Right, JINNY going to the door with them.

JINNY. [*Coming back from doorway.*] Now do tell me what it means. I thought you were abroad indefinitely, or for the summer at least.

MRS. CULLINGHAM. So did I! I'm just as surprised to be here as you seem to be! [*They sit down near each other.*] Didn't you really know we were coming?

JINNY. No! How should I?

MRS. CULLINGHAM. I don't know--I thought--

[*She hesitates, embarrassed.*

[*After a pause.*

JINNY. What did you think?

MRS. CULLINGHAM. Nothing, except that you must know we were coming home.

JINNY. Why--that *I* must?

MRS. CULLINGHAM. You mustn't put me into a corner like that!

JINNY. How do you mean "corner"? How did you happen to come home like this?

MRS. CULLINGHAM. Ruth suddenly got a cable--she didn't tell me from whom--but she said she must go home at once.

JINNY. But her mother's never been better!

MRS. CULLINGHAM. [*Carelessly.*] The cable wasn't from her mother.

JINNY. Oh, then, you know who it was from? [*No answer.*] Oh, I see now why you thought I ought to know about it; the cable was from *Jack*, *wasn't it*?

MRS. CULLINGHAM. [*Relieved.*] Yes.

JINNY. Oh, it was!

MRS. CULLINGHAM. I looked at it when she was out of the room; of course, it was sort of by accident-- [*Very much embarrassed.*] --that is, I just happened to see--O dear, there! You know what I mean; it was dreadful of me, but I couldn't help it.

JINNY. [*In a strained voice.*] Jack and Ruth are very good friends and he looks after some of her affairs. You know having no man in the family complicates things.

PETER. Oh! I say!

 [*Standing up, suddenly.*

MRS. CULLINGHAM. What *is it*, dear?

PETER. I believe I haven't got my before-dinner tabs.

MRS. CULLINGHAM. Oh, look carefully!

PETER. [*He looks in his right-hand pocket, takes out a bottle.*] Soda mints! [*From his left-hand pocket a box.*] Alkali powders! [*From third pocket a bottle.*] Charcoal tablets! [*From fourth pocket another bottle.] Dr. Man's Positive Cure! [*From fifth pocket a box.*] Bicarbonate soda!

MRS. CULLINGHAM. There's your other side pocket!

PETER. That's my saccharine [*Showing bottle.*] and my lithia tabs. [*Showing another bottle.*] We'll have to go, mother; I've left them home!

MRS. CULLINGHAM. We must go, anyway, my dear.

[*Rising.*

[*JINNY also rises.*

PETER. [*Suddenly claps his hand behind him and speaks joyfully.*] No, we needn't go after all; I forgot my hip pocket. Here they are!

[*Bringing them out.*

MRS. CULLINGHAM. We must go all the same! [*To JINNY.*] Sometimes I think he takes too much medicine stuff!

JINNY. I should think so! Peter, you ought to diet.

PETER. I can't! I've tried, and I lose my appetite right away!

MRS. CULLINGHAM. Good-by, dear. How long will you be in town?

JINNY. I don't know--several weeks, I imagine. Jack came home on some business, you know, and I don't think it's settled yet. Good-by.

[*To PETER.*

PETER. Good-by. You know you mustn't drink water with your meals; that's the great thing. So I drink only champagne.

[*He goes out Right.*

MRS. CULLINGHAM. [*Waits and speaks to JINNY with real feeling.*] I'm awfully ashamed of myself, and I hope I haven't made any trouble or fuss with my meddling. Don't let me!

JINNY. No, of course not.

[*With a strained smile.*

MRS. CULLINGHAM. I wish I could believe you.

JINNY. Well, *do*.

MRS. CULLINGHAM. Good-by.

[*She goes out Right.*

JINNY. Good-by. Where's that telegram that came for him a little while ago? [*Going to the desk at Right, and finding the telegram.*] Of course it's from her, saying that she's arrived. That's the trouble with telegrams; the address doesn't give the handwriting away. She must have sent it from the dock! Couldn't even wait till she was home! [She walks to the window and stands there a moment, then comes back, looking at her watch.] Nearly seven already, and no sign of him, and we must dress and dine--huh! I think I might as well tear up my theatre tickets! [She paces up and down the room, stopping now and then with each new thought that comes to her.] I wonder if he went down there to meet her--he must have known the boat; if he cabled her to come back, she must have cabled an answer and what boat she'd take! But no other telegram has come for Jack here to my knowledge--oh! of course, what am I thinking of, she sent *that one* to *his office* to-day; she was afraid he might have left before this one could get there, so she risked it here. Good Heavens! why am I maudling on like this to myself out loud? It's really nothing--Jack will *explain* once more that he *can't* explain, but that Ruth has "troubles," and I'll believe him again! But I won't! He promised me she should stay over there! [*Looks at her watch again.*] He's there, with her! *Nothing ever* kept him half as late down town as this! What a little fool I am!

[*GEOFFREY enters suddenly Right.*

JINNY. [*Cries out, joyfully.*] Geoffrey! [And rushing to him, embraces him.] You brute, you, not to come straight back to New York when you heard I was home! You dear old darling, you!

GEOFFREY. I couldn't, old girl; there were reasons--I don't have to tell you I wanted to.

JINNY. I don't know! Was there a pretty girl up there, Geof? I'm sure I shouldn't think her pretty if you were in love with her. I believe I shall be awfully jealous of your wife when you get one!

GEOFFREY. Rubbish! Hasn't Jack come back yet?

JINNY. "Come back" from where?

GEOFFREY. Brooklyn.

JINNY. Brooklyn! Why, he told me--what did he go there for?

GEOFFREY. [*Embarrassed.*] I don't know if you don't--

JINNY. You *do*!!

GEOFFREY. No--really--I--

JINNY. Oh, it's something to be concealed, then?

GEOFFREY. Hang it, Jinny! drop the subject. I thought he said he was going to Brooklyn; probably I was mistaken.

JINNY. [*Satirically.*] One is so apt to think just casually that every one's going to Brooklyn! [*Looks at her watch.*] Of course it's Brooklyn. [*Goes and looks at the telegram; turns.*] So you're going back on *me*, too, are you? You're going to *protect Jack* at *my* expense!

[*AUSTIN enters Right.*

AUSTIN. [*Absorbed.*] Good evening, Jinny dear.

JINNY. It's after seven!

AUSTIN. [*Pleasantly.*] Is it? Have you been waiting long, Geoffrey?

GEOFFREY. No, I've only just now come in.

JINNY. It's *I* who have done the waiting!

AUSTIN. I'm sorry, but it couldn't be helped.

JINNY. You didn't tell me you were going to Brooklyn.

AUSTIN. [After a quick, sharp look at Geoffrey, who shakes his head once emphatically.] It must have escaped my mind.

JINNY. That's very likely! Going to Brooklyn's the sort of thing one talks about and dreads for days.

AUSTIN. Well, Jinny, that will bear postponement, and my conversation with Geoffrey won't; will you please leave us together here for a while?

JINNY. And what about the theatre?

AUSTIN. What theatre?

JINNY. Oh, you've **forgotten** entirely my little birthday party! Thanks!

AUSTIN. Oh, Jinny! I **did**! Forgive me! I'm awfully sorry! I've got a lot on my mind to-day.

[Tries to put his arms about her and kiss her. She pushes herself away from him, refusing to let him kiss her.

JINNY. Yes--I know you have-- [**At door Left.**] --I'll leave you two to your confidences. You can trust Geof; he just now refused to betray you.

[AUSTIN only looks at her fixedly, seriously. She looks back at him with bravado. Then she deliberately crosses the room, gets the cable, and recrosses with it and goes out Left.

AUSTIN. Poor Jinny! [**Turning to GEOFFREY.**] and that, too, lies largely on your already overcrowded shoulders.

GEOFFREY. [**Breaking down.**] I know! I know!

AUSTIN. [*Sitting in the corner of the sofa.*] Here, don't cry! You've got to be strong now, and you've no use nor time for crying. I've had another long interview with the Brooklyn minister.

GEOFFREY. Yes?--

AUSTIN. [*Drawing a chair near to him and sitting.*] Well, of course we both know that he's doing wrong to keep silent, but he will. He wishes I hadn't told him, because he thinks he'd never have noticed your divorce from Maggie when it was granted--nor remembered your name if he had seen it in the papers.

GEOFFREY. That's what I *told* you!

AUSTIN. *You* only argued that for fear I'd insist on *your* going to this minister yourself. But in the bottom of your heart you know it was a risk we couldn't afford to run. I've explained everything to him--how such a fine, sweet girl would suffer if he did expose you, and I gave him my word you would be remarried to Ruth at once after the divorce. Of course we both know it's wrong, but we both hope the end justifies the means that removes difficulty number two.

GEOFFREY. You're sure about Maggie?

AUSTIN. She's signed a paper; she realizes you'll never live with her, and--it's pathetic--she loves you--that girl, too--so much as to give you your freedom--Good Lord! what is it about you weak men that wins women so? What is it in *you* that has made two women love *you* to such a self-sacrificing extent?

GEOFFREY. [*Half tragic, half comic laugh.*] I give it up!

AUSTIN. [*Bitterly.*] So do I. Well, Maggie is to have six hundred dollars a year.

GEOFFREY. Where'll I get it?

AUSTIN. We'll talk about that when the time comes. [*He rises.*] *Now* the most important, the most painful, task of all must be done and *you* must do it. *Not I this time--you!*

GEOFFREY. [*Looking up, frightened.*] What?

AUSTIN. Ruth Chester landed this morning.

GEOFFREY. [*Starting up.*] Impossible!

[*Rising.*

AUSTIN. The moment Maggie signed my paper I cabled Miss Chester to return. You can't go out west and institute proceedings for divorce without her *knowing the whole truth from you* first! You don't want her to find it out from the newspapers, do you?

GEOFFREY. And you want *me* to tell her?

AUSTIN. *To-day.* And to-morrow you start west!

GEOFFREY. [*Facing AUSTIN.*] I *won't* tell her!

AUSTIN. [*Calmly.*] You've got to!

Geoffrey. I'd rather shoot myself; do you understand me--I'd rather shoot myself!

AUSTIN. That's nothing! That would be decidedly the *easiest* course out of it, *and* the most *cowardly*.

GEOFFREY. She'll hate me! She'll loathe me! How could she help it at first! But just after a little, if I weren't there, the love she has for me might move her somehow or other--and by degrees perhaps--to forgive--

AUSTIN. I don't deny that you will have to go through a terrible degradation with her--but that is nothing compared with what you deserve. If *you* tell her, at least the humiliation is secret, locked there between you two, and no one else in the world can ever know what happens; *but* if you send some one else, and no matter who,--*any one* else but you *is* an outsider,--you ask her to make a spectacle of her humiliation, to let a third in as witness to the relations and emotions between you two! It's insulting her *again*! Don't you *see*?

  [*A pause.*

GEOFFREY. Yes, I see! My God! I *must* tell her myself.

AUSTIN. That's right, don't waver, make up your mind and do it--Come!

  [*Urging him up.*

GEOFFREY. [*Hesitates a moment.*] And Jinny?

AUSTIN. Oh, she'll come round all right; she always does.

GEOFFREY. And she doesn't suspect?

AUSTIN. Not the slightest.

[*A pause.*

GEOFFREY. Need she?

AUSTIN. The worst? No, **never**!

GEOFFREY. [*He rises, with new encouragement.*] You'll give me your word?

AUSTIN. Yes. [*Shakes his hand.*] I know how much she loves you; *I* wouldn't have her know anything. It's made us some ugly scenes, but they soon pass, and when you are once out of your trouble for good, we'll have no excuse, I'm sure, for any more!

GEOFFREY. Then I shall go to bed to-night with the respect still of at least two women who are dear to me, my mother and Jinny, even if I lose the respect and love of the one woman who is dearer! Only think, Jack, how I've got to stand up there--never mind about myself--and make her suffer tortures! Good-by. God give me courage to do the heart-breaking thing I must do.

AUSTIN. I am sure the one hope you have of forgiveness is in your manliness of going to her as you are doing and telling her yourself **all** the truth!

GEOFFREY. And that, like everything else, I owe to you.

AUSTIN. No, to *Jinny*! Good luck!

[*He shakes GEOFFREY'S hand and GEOFFREY goes out Right.*

AUSTIN. [Goes to the door Left, opens it, and calls to JINNY, in the next room.] Jinny, Geoffrey's gone,--what are you doing?

JINNY. [*Answers in a very little staccato voice.*] Waiting till you should have the leisure to receive me!

AUSTIN. Come along!

[*Leaves the doorway.*

[*JINNY enters Left and stands in the doorway.*

JINNY. [*With affected nonchalance.*] I didn't care to go downstairs for dinner, so I have had a tray up here. Maggie brought up something for you, too; would you like it now?

AUSTIN. [*Ignoring purposely her mood and manner.*] I shouldn't mind! I do feel a little hungry.

[*He sits in the arm-chair.*

JINNY. [*Speaks off through the doorway Left.*] Bring in the tray for Mr. Austin, Maggie.

MAGGIE. [*Off stage.*] Yes'm.

[JINNY pulls forward a little tea table beside his chair. Her whole manner must be one of slow, dragging carelessness, like the calm before a storm. Her expression must be hard. She carries the telegram still unopened, and on top of it the theatre tickets torn into pieces.

[MAGGIE brings in the tray, puts it on the table, and goes out Right.

On the tray are chops, peas, some whiskey, a syphon, a roll, etc.

AUSTIN. [*Sits down quickly and with a show of eagerness.*] Ah!

[*Begins to eat as if he were hungry and enjoyed it.*

[JINNY sits on the sofa at his Left, and looks at him,--AUSTIN is of course conscious of JINNY'S mood, but pretends not to notice it.

AUSTIN. [*After a silence during which he eats.*] I say I *am* hungry! And these chops *are* very good, aren't they?

[*No answer.*

I'll tell you what it is, Jinny! Of course travelling is great sport and all the rest of it, but after all one does get tired of hotels, and to quote a somewhat familiar refrain, "There's no place like home."

[*No answer.*

Have you a headache, Jinny?

JINNY. [*Very short.*] No.

AUSTIN. That's a good thing, and I hope you are not as disappointed as I am about the theatre.

JINNY. [*Half laughs.*] Humph!

AUSTIN. I'll celebrate *your* birthday to-morrow and take *you*.

JINNY. [*Quickly.*] *Why* did you go to Brooklyn?

AUSTIN. On the private business of some one else.

JINNY. [*With all her nerves tied tight.*] That's the best answer you will give me?

AUSTIN. My dear girl, it's the only answer I *can* give you.

JINNY. When you are through I have something for you!

AUSTIN. What?

JINNY. I'll give it to you when you have finished.

AUSTIN. I'm ready. [He rises. JINNY rises too, and gives him the telegram with the torn tickets on top, and then rings the bell, at Right.] What are these torn papers?

JINNY. Our theatre tickets!

[*He looks at her.*

AUSTIN. And when did this telegram come?

JINNY. This afternoon.

AUSTIN. Why didn't I get it when I came in?

JINNY. [*Bitingly.*] I kept it to have the *pleasure* of giving it to you myself; it's from Ruth Chester.

AUSTIN. How do you know?

JINNY. Oh, I haven't opened it! But I know! When I held it in my hand it burnt my fingers! [*MAGGIE enters Right.*] Take away the tray, please, Maggie.

MAGGIE. Yes'm.

[*She leaves the room with the tray.*

[*JINNY replaces the small table carelessly, almost roughly.*

[*AUSTIN opens and reads the telegram; there is a second's pause.*

JINNY. May I read it?

AUSTIN. [*After a moment's hesitation.*] Yes, if you wish.

[*Not handing it to her.*

JINNY. I *do*!

AUSTIN. [*Reaches over and hands her the telegram; he speaks quietly.*] When you behave like this it's impossible for me to feel the same toward you.

JINNY. And how do you think I feel when I read this?

[*Reads it, satirically, bitterly.*

"Arrived safely; please let me see you before the day goes. Ruth."
"*Ruth*" if you please!

AUSTIN. [*Standing over JINNY.*] I want you to be careful to-night. I want you to control yourself. I've been through a great deal to-day, and if you make me angry God knows what I mightn't say and *do*!

JINNY. And *I've* been through a great deal *for many a day now*, and I want the truth about this at last! It's all very well for you to spare her by not telling me what this *mysterious* trouble is about which you've been hoodwinking me ever since we were married, but *now* you've got to choose between sparing *her* and sparing *me*!

[*She sits determinedly.*

AUSTIN. Is this your answer to me when I beg you to be very careful to-night to control yourself?

JINNY. It's your turn to be careful! What did you marry me for if you were in love with Ruth?

AUSTIN. *Jinny!*

JINNY. [*A little frightened, to excuse herself.*] You gave me your word of honor she would stay abroad indefinitely.

AUSTIN. Nonsense! I said I understood she was going to stay some time--indefinitely.

JINNY. It's the same thing, and here she is back practically the moment we are!

AUSTIN. I can't control Miss Chester's movements--I couldn't foresee when she would come back. In Rome she told me she would stay on.

JINNY. [*Rising and facing him.*] Ah! that's what I wanted to see, if you really *would lie* to me!

AUSTIN. What do you mean?

JINNY. [*Beside herself.*] Liar! [He only looks at her, with his face hard and set; she is insane with jealousy for the moment.] *You sent* for Ruth to come back.

AUSTIN. *And* if *I did*?

JINNY. You tried to deceive me about it. And if you'll tell me a lie about one thing, you'll tell me a lie about another, and I don't believe one word of all your explanations about the intrigue between you and Ruth Chester!

AUSTIN. [*Taking her two hands.*] Sit down!

  [*She sits in the arm-chair, half forced by him.*

JINNY. *Why* did you send for Ruth Chester to come back?

AUSTIN. I have told you before, I am trying to help Miss Chester.

JINNY. "*Ruth!*"

AUSTIN. I am trying to help her in a great and serious trouble.

JINNY. Why did you send for her to come back? What's the trouble?

AUSTIN. I've told you before I can't tell you.

JINNY. You daren't tell me, and you haven't even the face to tell another lie about it!

AUSTIN. If you say another word, I shall *hate* you! If you *won't* control *yourself*, I must make you, as well as keep my own sane balance. You have insulted my love for you to-night as you've never done before; you've struck at my own ideal of *you*; you've almost done, in a word, what I warned you you might do--*kill* the love I have for you!

JINNY. [*Frightened.*] Jack!

AUSTIN. I mean what I say!

JINNY. [*In tears.*] That--that you--you don't love me?

AUSTIN. That is not what I said, but I tell you now that since I first began to care for you, never have I loved you so little as I do to-night.

JINNY. [*With an effort at angry justification.*] And suppose I tell you it is your own fault, because you haven't treated me--

AUSTIN. [*Interrupting her.*] Like a *child*, instead of a *woman*!

JINNY. No, because you've kept part of yourself from me, and that part you've given--

AUSTIN. For God's sake, stop! [A pause--JINNY is now thoroughly frightened; slowly she comes to her senses.] Do you *want* a rupture for good between us? [*No answer.*] Can't you see what I tell you is true? That I can't bear any more to-night? That if you keep on you will rob *me* of every bit of love I have for you, just as you've already robbed me of the woman I thought you were?

JINNY. "Already!" No, no, Jack, don't say that. Oh, what have I done!

[*She cries.*

AUSTIN. You've done something very serious, and before you do more-- [*Speaking hardly.*] --I think we'd better not stay in this evening; it would be wiser for both of us if we went out somewhere.

JINNY. No, I couldn't go out feeling this way! I've hurt you, hurt you terribly! Oh, why do I do it? Why can't I help myself?

AUSTIN. I think one more scene to-night would finish things for us. I *warn* you of that, Jinny--

[He goes to the desk and sits at it, looking blankly before him. She comes slowly, almost timidly, behind his chair.

JINNY. No, don't say it! don't say it! Try to forgive me--oh, Jack, I hate myself, and I'm so ashamed of myself! I know I've disappointed you awfully, awfully! You *did* idealize me; I knew it when you married me, but I told you then I wasn't worth your loving me, didn't I? I never pretended to be worthy of you. I always knew I wasn't.

AUSTIN. Hush!

JINNY. It's true! it's only too awfully true. But do you remember how you answered me then when I told you I wasn't worth your loving me?

AUSTIN. [*Coldly and without looking at her.*] No.

JINNY. You took me in your arms and held me so I couldn't have got away if I'd wanted to--which I didn't--and stopped the words on my lips with your *kisses.* [Her throat fills. He makes no reply. She goes on very pathetically.] *How I wish* you'd answer me that way now!

AUSTIN. Whose fault is it?

JINNY. Oh, mine! *mine*! I know it. *You* don't know it one-half so well as I! I love you better than anything in the world, love everything of you--the turn of your head, the blessed touch of your hand, the smallest word that comes from your dear lips--the thoughts that your forehead hides, but which my heart guesses when I'm sane! And yet, try as hard as I can, these mad fits take hold of me, and although I'd willingly *die* to save you *pain*, still *I*, *I* myself, hurt and wound you past all bearing! It doesn't make any difference that *I* suffer too! *I ought* to! I deserve to--you *don't*! Oh, no! I know I'm a disappointment and a failure!

 [*Her eyes fill up with tears and her voice breaks.*

AUSTIN. [*He turns to her.*] No, Jinny, not so bad as that, only I thought you were *big*--and you're *so little*, oh, *so small*!

JINNY. Yes, it's true; I'm small--I'm *small*! Oh, I'd like to be big, too! I want to be noble and strong, but I'm not--I'm as weak as water--only it's *boiling* water! I want to be Brunhilde, and I'm only Frou Frou! Yes, I'm little; but I *love* you--*I love you!*

 [*She sinks on to a stool beside him. A moment's pause.*

 [*With a trembling voice.*

You don't mind my sitting here?

AUSTIN. No--

 [Very quietly, he places his arm about her neck, his hand on her shoulder. She quickly steals up her hand to take his, and leaning her head over it, kisses his hand. He draws it away and kisses her hair.

JINNY. [*Timidly, very softly.*] You forgive me?

AUSTIN. [*With a long sigh.*] Yes.

JINNY. [*Bursting into tears and burying her face upon his knees.*] Thank you--thank you--I know I don't deserve it--I don't deserve it--I don't deserve it!

AUSTIN. [*Softly.*] Sh!--

[*JINNY half turns and looks up at him.*

JINNY. [*Very, very quietly.*] You forgive me--but still--yes, I see it in your face, you don't love me the same. You look so tired, dear.

AUSTIN. [*Also very quietly.*] I am, Jinny.

JINNY. And--happy?

AUSTIN. I'm *not* quite happy.

JINNY. I wish I could make you so--make you love me the old way. You used to smile a little when you looked at me--Jack, you don't any more. But I mean to make you to-night, if I can, and to make you love me as much as ever you did.

AUSTIN. Good luck, dear.

JINNY. [*Brightening.*] What time is it?

AUSTIN. [*Looking at his watch.*] Nearly nine.

JINNY. I suppose it is too late for me to dress and for us to go to the theatre?

AUSTIN. Oh, yes,--and I'm too tired.

JINNY. [*Triumphantly.*] Well, then, you shall have your theatre at home! If Mahomet won't go to the mountain, the mountain must go to your lordship!

AUSTIN. I don't understand!

JINNY. Well, just wait-- [*She blows her nose.*] --till I bathe my face and eyes a little; I feel rather bleary! [Starting to go, she stops and turns.] Good-by?

   [*Questioningly.*

AUSTIN. [*Quietly.*] Good-by.

JINNY. [*Who wanted him to call her to him and kiss her.*] Oh, very well! but I'll *make* you smile yet and *kiss* me of your own accord to-night--you'll see!

   [*She goes out Left.*

[She is heard singing in her room. AUSTIN goes to the desk and after a long sigh he begins to write.]

AUSTIN. [*Writing.*] Dear Ruth. The satisfaction of the visit to Brooklyn prevents me from being disappointed at having missed your telegram till too late to go to your house to-night. My heart aches for the blow you must have this evening, but please God you will bear it bravely. The man who loves you is not bad, but he has been weak. However, I feel once he can shake off the burden of his present marriage, you will never have cause to complain of him again. And if your future happiness lies truly in his hands, it will be safe there.

JINNY. [*Calls from her room.*] Are you ready?

AUSTIN. Yes.

[*He stops writing.*

JINNY. In your orchestra chair?

AUSTIN. Yes.

JINNY. What will you have, tragedy or comedy?

AUSTIN. [*Smiling.*] Shall we begin with tragedy?

JINNY. All right.

AUSTIN. [*Continues to write.*] So far I have been able to keep Jinny in absolute ignorance, but I fear the blow must fall upon her soon, and I dread to think of what she, too, will suffer. Help me to keep it from her as long as we can, won't you?

[JINNY comes back; she has changed her dress to a loose negligee gown, with a red turban on her head; she brings two sheets with her.

JINNY. Excuse me one minute while I set the stage! [Moving toward each other the big arm-chair and the sofa, she covers them with the sheets. AUSTIN turns from his letter on the desk, to watch.] Uncle Tom's Cabin, Act Four! [She goes out only for a moment, and reenters, wearing a man's overcoat, with a pillow tied in the middle with a silk scarf, eyes, nose, and mouth made on it with a burnt match.] Eliza crossing the ice! Come, honey darling! [*To the pillow.*] Mammy'll save you from de wicked white man! [Jumping up on the sofa, and moving with the springs.] *You* ought to do the bloodhounds for me, Jack! Excuse me, but you look the part! [AUSTIN watches her, not unamused, but without smiling.] Hold tight to Lize, honey, and don't be afeerd o' dat big black man over dah--dat's Uncle Tom. [*Crossing to the arm-chair.*] Don't be afeerd, honey; it's Lize dat's cuttin' de ice this time. [She throws the pillow away and drags off the two sheets.] Oh, I can see this is too serious for you!

[She starts singing a cakewalk and dances across the room until she reaches him, where she finishes.

AUSTIN. Very good, Jinny! I'm sure we couldn't have seen better at the theatre.

JINNY. Ah! You're getting yourself again!--Darling! Come!--Come!--come to the pianola and you shall have the sextette! It's in there ready; I heard mother struggling with it. You don't suppose she has designs upon the Casino, do you? Now--ready?

[He goes to the pianola and starts to play the sextette from "Florodora." She runs to the opposite side of the room and begins to sing and dance, crossing to AUSTIN as he plays.

AUSTIN. [*After a few moments.*] But I can't see you and play at the same time; I don't like it!

JINNY. [*Delighted.*] You *want to see me*, do you?

AUSTIN. Of course I do!

JINNY. Jack! [*Delighted.*] Well, then, turn round!

[JINNY, hurrying the time of the song, turns it into a regular skirt dance. She dances delightfully and AUSTIN cannot resist her charm. His face lightens, he smiles, and love comes into his eyes. JINNY sees and dances and sings all the better till she reaches him.

AUSTIN. [*Rising, he takes her into his arms.*] You adorable Jinny!

JINNY. Ah, Jack! You're smiling again and--*you love me*!

 [*Clasping her arms about his neck.*

AUSTIN. Yes! Is the theatre finished?

JINNY. No, only the first act. [He sits in the big arm-chair, JINNY on his knee.] I'm *tired*! [He kisses her. There is a pause. There is a knock on the door at Right.] Oh, hang it! [*Knock repeated.*] *Don't* answer it! We haven't half made up yet!

AUSTIN. But we must answer it, dear.

JINNY. [*As she rises unwillingly.*] I don't see why--I should have let her knock till she went away.

AUSTIN. Come in!

[*MAGGIE enters with a letter.*

JINNY. What is it, Maggie?

MAGGIE. A note from Miss Chester, m'm, and she's downstairs herself waiting for an answer.

JINNY. For *me*?

[*Taking the letter.*

MAGGIE. No, m'm; I think she said it was for *Mr.* Austin.

JINNY. *Oh!*--You may wait outside for the answer, Maggie.

MAGGIE. Yes, m'm.

[*She goes out.*

JINNY. [*Slowly goes to AUSTIN and gives him the letter, lightly.*] I see now why you were so anxious to let Maggie in. Perhaps you were expecting this.

AUSTIN. Jinny! [Holding her by the hand and trying to pull her over to him.] Come, I'll give you a kiss for the letter.

JINNY. No, thank you, I don't want kisses that are given by you for letters from Ruth Chester. Yes! do kiss me! [*He kisses her.*] I *won't* be jealous! *I won't be!* [*Clinching her teeth.*] See, I'm not jealous a bit! Read your old letter!

[AUSTIN opens the note and reads it. As he does so JINNY has passed on to the desk and sees AUSTIN'S unfinished letter to RUTH, which after a little hesitation she picks up and reads. AUSTIN, having read RUTH'S note, looks up thoughtfully a second, and then re-reads it. JINNY is furious over what she reads. As she finishes she gives a little cry from the very depths of her heart.

JINNY. Oh, *Jack*!

AUSTIN. What is it?

JINNY. Nothing!

[She sinks by the desk, crushing the letter in her hand. She looks over at him, and then down at the letter, and then back at him.

AUSTIN. Maggie!

JINNY. [Rising suddenly. She speaks with a voice trembling with only half-contained emotion and passion.] I told her to wait in the hall; may I read it?

  [*Holding out her hand for the letter.*

AUSTIN. Now look here, Jinny,--I always let you read everything, don't I?

JINNY. [*Hiding his letter behind her back.*] Yes. [Holding out her other hand.] Give it to me!

AUSTIN. Now begin to show that you really are going to turn over a new leaf, and that your love is going to have perfect confidence, and don't ask to see this letter.

JINNY. But I *do* ask to see it!

AUSTIN. Then this time I must refuse you!

JINNY. What! is it even more compromising than *your* letter to her?

AUSTIN. What letter? [Looking first on the desk, he looks across at her and sees it in her hand. He is angry, but also frightened for fear it has told her her brother's secret.] And you've read it?

JINNY. It lay open on the desk there, and anyway the end justifies me!

AUSTIN. [*In an agony.*] What does it tell you? I forget what I wrote!

JINNY. It tells me that my jealousy all along has been right, that I've been a fool to let you blind me!

AUSTIN. [*With a great sigh of relief.*] Is that all?

JINNY. [*Beside herself.*] "Is that all!" Isn't that enough? Dear God, isn't that enough? That there's an understanding between you and Ruth to get rid of *me*!

AUSTIN. If it tells you that, the letter lies! Give it to me!

JINNY. No! *I'll* read it to you! [*Reads with bitter emphasis.*] "The satisfaction of the visit to Brooklyn prevents me from being disappointed at having missed your telegram till too late to go to your house to-night!" So--you and she went to Brooklyn, did you, and that's why you came back too late to go to the theatre with me? You *cheat*! [*She screams in her madness. A pause.*] Why don't you answer--why don't you say something?

AUSTIN. Because if I speak as I feel, I'm afraid of saying something I'll regret all my life!

JINNY. You don't deny, then?

AUSTIN. Yes! that is due to Ruth. Whatever you may feel about *me*, you have no *right* to *insult* her!

JINNY. Oh, *there's more to* the letter!

AUSTIN. Jinny, don't you see what you're doing?

JINNY. Yes, I'm getting at the truth at last! [*Reads.*] "My heart aches for the blow you must have this evening! The man who loves you--"

AUSTIN. You shan't read any more; you're mad now!

[*Tearing the letter away from her.*

JINNY. I don't need the letter, the words are burning in here! [*Pressing her hands to her forehead.*] "The man who loves you isn't bad, only weak. However, I feel once we can shake off the burden of *this present marriage*"--oh! you--you *brute* to say that!--"you will never have cause to complain of him again! So far I have been able to keep Jinny in perfect ignorance, but I feel the blow must fall upon her now--"

[*Interrupted.*

AUSTIN. Shall I tell you *the truth*?

JINNY. You don't have to; I've found it out for myself!

AUSTIN. [*In weariness, in disgust, in utter hopelessness.*] No! what's the use. You've done it now--let it go! Let it all go--the whole thing! What's the use!--it's finished!-- [*A knock on the door at Right.*] Come in!

[*Maggie enters and closes the door behind her.*

MAGGIE. Please, sir, Miss Chester came upstairs and made me knock again to see if there was an answer and if you will see her now or not.

JINNY. [*Suddenly--aflame with her idea.*] Yes! Maggie, show her in!

AUSTIN. No, no! What do you want to do! I'll see Miss Chester to-morrow, Maggie.

[*JINNY has crossed to the door, Right.*

JINNY. Ruth! Ruth!

RUTH. [*Off stage.*] Yes? May I come?

JINNY. *Do* come in!

[*She recrosses room; she and AUSTIN face each other for a second.*

AUSTIN. [*In a lowered voice.*] For God's sake, be careful!

[*RUTH enters Right.*

RUTH. Jinny!

[*Going to her quickly to embrace her.*

[JINNY, without speaking, draws away and stares at her with a look
of hatred. RUTH, seeing it, stops short, and looks from JINNY to
AUSTIN for explanation--she turns to AUSTIN and gives him her hand,
which he takes, presses, and drops; JINNY'S shoulders contract at
this moment; RUTH immediately turns again to JINNY.

RUTH. What is it, Jinny? [*To AUSTIN.*] Surely she doesn't blame *me* in
any way.

JINNY. *Blame you!*

AUSTIN. She doesn't *know*.

JINNY. That's a lie! I know everything, Ruth! I know why you followed my
husband to Rome, and why he sent for you to come back here. I know that
you and he were in Brooklyn this afternoon, and that you only plan to
get rid of me by some divorce, and by hook or crook to marry each other!

RUTH. No!--No!--

JINNY. Oh, you can lie, too, can you? I won't keep you waiting long!
You've stolen my husband from me--take him. I won't *share* him with any
woman! He's yours now, and I'll soon be out of your way!

AUSTIN. *Jinny!*

RUTH. [*To Austin.*] She must be told the truth.

[*AUSTIN bows his head.*

JINNY. Now you'll make up your story, will you? I tell you it's useless.
If he wouldn't let me see your compromising letter, I've seen a letter
from *him* to *you* to-night that gives the whole thing away.

RUTH. [*Very quietly.*] Your husband went to Brooklyn **without me**, as your **brother** will tell you, to see the clergyman who married me, or **thought** he **married** me to **Geoffrey Tillman** three months ago! [*JINNY looks up with a start.*] That marriage was **illegal** because your brother was already married, and Mr. Austin tried and did get the promise of silence this afternoon about the Brooklyn service, to prevent a charge of bigamy against your brother. The first marriage, which still holds good, was with--Maggie, your present servant--

[*JINNY stands immovable. There is a silence.*

AUSTIN. Geoffrey is not at your house?

RUTH. No, he left when I came on here. As I wrote you in the note I sent upstairs, I was too stunned by what he told me to answer then, and I wanted a word of advice with you. [*She turns to JINNY.*] *I* knew what I thought was my **marriage** to your brother must be kept secret, but I could not learn why. This was my trouble, which, after your marriage, I selfishly laid on your husband's shoulders, thinking he might help me! [*No answer from JINNY, who stands as if struck dumb and into stone.*] Mr. Austin only learned the whole truth when we met that day in Rome. *I* did not learn till to-day that I was not honestly your brother's wife. I had to be told, because divorce proceedings are to be started at once to break--the other--marriage. [*No answer from JINNY.*] To spare me, and above all to spare you the knowledge of your brother's sin, your husband has kept Geoffrey's secret from you. You have **well** repaid him! [*She turns again to AUSTIN.*] Good-by--I feel to-night I couldn't marry Geoffrey again. He's tumbled so far off his pedestal he has fallen out of my heart. But still--we'll see; I've told him to come to-morrow. *Thank you* from the bottom of my heart--it's full of gratitude, even if it is broken!

[*She goes out Right.*

[JINNY slowly turns, almost afraid to look at AUSTIN. He stands stern, with set face.

JINNY. [*In a low voice, ashamed to go near him.*] Can you forgive me? Can you--

AUSTIN. Ugh!

[*Crossing room for his coat.*

JINNY. I'm mad! You know I don't know what I do. But I *love you*--I love you! Forgive me!

AUSTIN. Never!

[*Taking up his coat.*

JINNY. Where are you going?

AUSTIN. Out of this house.

JINNY. If you leave me, I'll not bear it! I'll kill myself! I warn you!

AUSTIN. Bah!--Good-by!

[*Going to the door Right.*

JINNY. No! Where are you going?

AUSTIN. Out of this house *for good*!

[*At the door he turns and looks at her.*

JINNY. [*Echoes.*] For good?

AUSTIN. *For good!*

[*He goes out, slamming the door behind him.*

[JINNY stands a moment motionless. She then cries faintly--"Jack!"
She goes to the door and pushes it open, crying out again in loud,
strong despair, "Jack!" There is a moment's pause. She cries out
again weakly, heartbrokenly, "Jack!"--comes back into the room, and
throwing herself down on the floor, her head resting on her arms in
the arm-chair, she sobs hysterically, wildly, "What have I done! Dear
God, what have I done!" as

THE CURTAIN FALLS

ACT IV

Scene I

Dawn of the next day. At the rise of the curtain JINNY is by the open window, whose curtains she has thrown aside. The sky is blood-red and streaked with gold the moment before sunrise. JINNY is worn and haggard, with hair dishevelled.

JINNY. [*Turning and leaning against the window.*] Day at last! What a night--what a night--but now it's morning and he hasn't come back! He means it! And it's my own fault--it's my own fault! [She shivers. She closes the window and comes away. After a moment's pause she goes deliberately and looks at the several gas fixtures in the room. She then closes all the doors and locks them. She carefully draws down the shade and closes in the curtains of the window. She hesitates, then pulls aside the curtains and the shade, and takes a long, last look at the dawn. She closes it all in again. She gets Austin's picture from the desk and places it on the table near the centre of the room. She then goes to the gas bracket at the Right and turns on the gas. She lights it to see if the gas is all right; then blows it out. She then crosses to the other bracket and turns that on; she goes to the chandelier at centre, and, mounting a chair, turns on its three jets. She then sits down by the table with AUSTIN'S picture before her, and looking into its eyes, her elbows on the table, her head in her hands, she waits.] Oh,

Jack, my beloved! I couldn't help it--I never for one minute stopped loving you better than everything else in my life, but no more than I could stop loving you could I stop or help being jealous! Once the cruel idea has got hold of me it seems to *have* to work its way out! Everything gets red before me and I don't seem to know what I say or do! It's no excuse, I know. I've got no excuse, only I *love* you! You'll forgive me when I'm gone, won't you, Jack? You'll know I *loved* you!--loved you so I couldn't *live* without you!--loved you!--*loved* you! [She kisses the photograph tenderly, adoringly, slowly, in tears.] Loved--you--loved you!--loved--

[*Her head drops forward, as*

THE CURTAIN FALLS

SCENE II

The same morning, three hours later. The curtain rises on the same scene in a dull, cold, early morning light. The lamp has burnt itself out. A tiny ray of sunlight steals through a slip between the curtains. JINNY sits by the table, her arms spread over it and her head on her arms--she is perfectly still. AUSTIN'S picture is before her. There is a moment's silence. Voices are heard outside, approaching door, at Right. Gradually what they say is distinguished.

MAGGIE. No, sir. She hasn't been to bed; I've been to her bedroom--that door's not unlocked.

TILLMAN. She's been here all night?

MAGGIE. Yes, sir. But twice in the night, sir, I came to the door and spoke to her and she wouldn't answer me--but I could hear her walking up and down and sometimes talking to herself.

TILLMAN. [*Calls softly.*] Jinny! [*Knocks softly.*] It's father! [No answer.] It looks as if she were asleep now.

AUSTIN. [*At a little distance.*] Father!

TILLMAN. I'm outside the library door.

AUSTIN. [*Nearer.*] I can't wait--have you seen her? Will she see me?

TILLMAN. She's locked herself in here. She's not been to her own room.

AUSTIN. Not been to bed at all! Poor Jinny--God forgive me.

TILLMAN. Maggie says she's walked the floor all night.

[*He knocks on the door Right.*

AUSTIN. [*Outside the door, Right, rather softly.*] Jinny! I'm so sorry! I can't say how sorry! I've thought it out through the night, and I think I understand things better. [*He waits a moment for an answer.*] Jinny, answer me! you shall be as jealous as you like, and I'll always explain and kiss away those doubts of yours, and I'll have no more secrets from you, dear. Not one! Jinny! [As he calls there is a slight movement of one of JINNY'S arms. With a note of alarm.] Father! I can't hear a sound of breathing! [*A moment's pause as they listen.*] She threatened it--she threatened it several times! [With great determination.] We must get into this room--do you hear me--we must get in if we have to break the door down! [They shake the door. He calls a little louder.] Jinny, Jinny darling--do you hear me? [JINNY makes a sort of feeble effort to lift her head, but fails.] Jinny, for God's sake, answer me! I love you Jinny--***Jinny!*** [Very slowly JINNY lifts her head and, with difficulty, she hears as if in a dream; she is dazed, barely alive.] She doesn't answer!

TILLMAN. See if the key is in the lock.

AUSTIN. No.

TILLMAN. Get the other keys, Maggie.

AUSTIN. ***Father!*** Gas! Don't you smell it?

TILLMAN. What!

AUSTIN. Gas, I tell you! O God! she's killed herself! Jinny! Jinny!

[***Beating the door.***

[JINNY staggers up, she tries to call "Jack"--but the word only comes out in a half-articulate whisper! She tries again, but fails.

MAGGIE. Here's a key, sir.

[JINNY tries to go to the door; she staggers a few steps and then falls.

[***They try one key--it does not unlock the door; they try another.***

[JINNY half raises herself and makes an effort to crawl, but is unable and sinks back upon the floor.

AUSTIN. Break the door in, father! We daren't waste any more time!

TILLMAN. No, this has done it!

[They open the door and rush in. They stop aghast at JINNY and the oppressiveness of the gas in the room.

TILLMAN. Jinny!

AUSTIN. Quick--the window! [TILLMAN tears aside the curtains and throws open the window. The sunshine of full morning pours in. He then rushes to the opposite gas burners and turns them off. Kneeling quickly beside her.] *Jinny! My wife!* My beloved!

[*He takes her up in his arms and hurries to the window.*

TILLMAN. Are we too late?

AUSTIN. I don't know. No! she's breathing--and see--see!--she knows me!--she knows me! [*JINNY smiles at him pathetically.*] Send Maggie for the doctor!

[*TILLMAN goes out Right.*

AUSTIN. Jinny, forgive me! Forgive me! Forgive me! [She slips her two arms up and joins them about his neck. AUSTIN kisses her.] Father! We've saved her! Oh, thank God, we've saved her!

[Bringing her to big chair and putting her in it, he kneels at her feet.

JINNY. [*Whispers faintly.*] *Dear Jack!* You forgive *me*--all my beastly jealousy?

AUSTIN. There's one thing stronger even than jealousy, my Jinny. And that's LOVE! That's *LOVE*!

[*He kisses her hands, and*

www.bookjungle.com *email: sales@bookjungle.com fax: 630-214-0564 mail: Book Jungle PO Box 2226 Champaign, IL 61825*

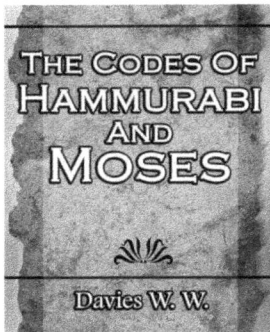

The Codes Of Hammurabi And Moses
W. W. Davies

QTY

The discovery of the Hammurabi Code is one of the greatest achievements of archaeology, and is of paramount interest, not only to the student of the Bible, but also to all those interested in ancient history...

Religion   **ISBN:** *1-59462-338-4*   **Pages:132**
MSRP $12.95

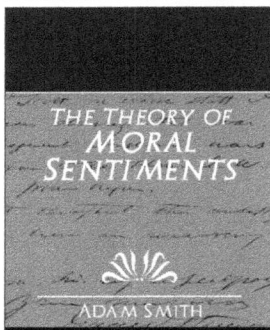

The Theory of Moral Sentiments
Adam Smith

QTY

This work from 1749. contains original theories of conscience amd moral judgment and it is the foundation for systemof morals.

Philosophy ISBN: *1-59462-777-0*   **Pages:536**
MSRP $19.95

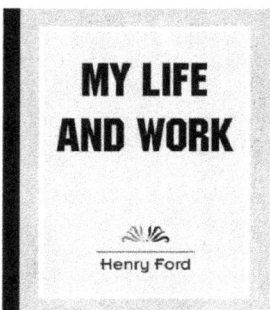

Jessica's First Prayer
Hesba Stretton

QTY

In a screened and secluded corner of one of the many railway-bridges which span the streets of London there could be seen a few years ago, from five o'clock every morning until half past eight, a tidily set-out coffee-stall, consisting of a trestle and board, upon which stood two large tin cans, with a small fire of charcoal burning under each so as to keep the coffee boiling during the early hours of the morning when the work-people were thronging into the city on their way to their daily toil...

Pages:84

Childrens   ISBN: *1-59462-373-2*   *MSRP $9.95*

My Life and Work
Henry Ford

QTY

Henry Ford revolutionized the world with his implementation of mass production for the Model T automobile. Gain valuable business insight into his life and work with his own auto-biography... "We have only started on our development of our country we have not as yet, with all our talk of wonderful progress, done more than scratch the surface. The progress has been wonderful enough but..."

Pages:300

Biographies/   ISBN: *1-59462-198-5*   *MSRP $21.95*

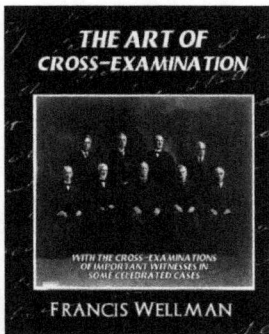

The Art of Cross-Examination
Francis Wellman

QTY

I presume it is the experience of every author, after his first book is published upon an important subject, to be almost overwhelmed with a wealth of ideas and illustrations which could readily have been included in his book, and which to his own mind, at least, seem to make a second edition inevitable. Such certainly was the case with me; and when the first edition had reached its sixth impression in five months, I rejoiced to learn that it seemed to my publishers that the book had met with a sufficiently favorable reception to justify a second and considerably enlarged edition. ..

Pages:412

Reference   ISBN: *1-59462-647-2*   *MSRP $19.95*

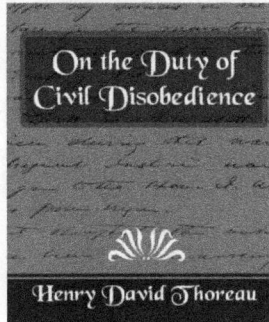

On the Duty of Civil Disobedience
Henry David Thoreau

QTY

Thoreau wrote his famous essay, On the Duty of Civil Disobedience, as a protest against an unjust but popular war and the immoral but popular institution of slave-owning. He did more than write—he declined to pay his taxes, and was hauled off to gaol in consequence. Who can say how much this refusal of his hastened the end of the war and of slavery ?

Law   ISBN: *1-59462-747-9*   **Pages:48**

MSRP $7.45

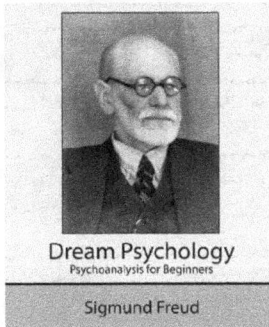

Dream Psychology Psychoanalysis for Beginners
Sigmund Freud

QTY

Sigmund Freud, born Sigismund Schlomo Freud (May 6, 1856 - September 23, 1939), was a Jewish-Austrian neurologist and psychiatrist who co-founded the psychoanalytic school of psychology. Freud is best known for his theories of the unconscious mind, especially involving the mechanism of repression; his redefinition of sexual desire as mobile and directed towards a wide variety of objects; and his therapeutic techniques, especially his understanding of transference in the therapeutic relationship and the presumed value of dreams as sources of insight into unconscious desires.

Pages:196

Psychology   ISBN: *1-59462-905-6*   *MSRP $15.45*

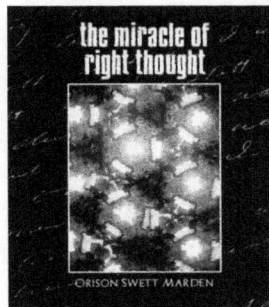

The Miracle of Right Thought
Orison Swett Marden

QTY

Believe with all of your heart that you will do what you were made to do. When the mind has once formed the habit of holding cheerful, happy, prosperous pictures, it will not be easy to form the opposite habit. It does not matter how improbable or how far away this realization may see, or how dark the prospects may be, if we visualize them as best we can, as vividly as possible, hold tenaciously to them and vigorously struggle to attain them, they will gradually become actualized, realized in the life. But a desire, a longing without endeavor, a yearning abandoned or held indifferently will vanish without realization.

Pages:360

Self Help   ISBN: *1-59462-644-8*   *MSRP $25.45*

QTY

The Rosicrucian Cosmo-Conception Mystic Christianity *by Max Heindel* ISBN: *1-59462-188-8* **$38.95**
The Rosicrucian Cosmo-conception is not dogmatic, neither does it appeal to any other authority than the reason of the student. It is: not controversial, but is: sent forth in the, hope that it may help to clear... New Age/Religion Pages 646

Abandonment To Divine Providence *by Jean-Pierre de Caussade* ISBN: *1-59462-228-0* **$25.95**
"The Rev. Jean Pierre de Caussade was one of the most remarkable spiritual writers of the Society of Jesus in France in the 18th Century. His death took place at Toulouse in 1751. His works have gone through many editions and have been republished... Inspirational/Religion Pages 400

Mental Chemistry *by Charles Haanel* ISBN: *1-59462-192-6* **$23.95**
Mental Chemistry allows the change of material conditions by combining and appropriately utilizing the power of the mind. Much like applied chemistry creates something new and unique out of careful combinations of chemicals the mastery of mental chemistry.., New Age Pages 354

The Letters of Robert Browning and Elizabeth Barret Barrett 1845-1846 vol II ISBN: *1-59462-193-4* **$35.95**
by Robert Browning and Elizabeth Barrett Biographies Pages 596

Gleanings In Genesis (volume I) *by Arthur W. Pink* ISBN: *1-59462-130-6* **$27.45**
Appropriately has Genesis been termed "the seed plot of the Bible" for in it we have, in germ form, almost all of the great doctrines which are afterwards fully developed in the books of Scripture which follow... Religion/Inspirational Pages 420

The Master Key *by L. W. de Laurence* ISBN: *1-59462-001-6* **$30.95**
In no branch of human knowledge has there been a more lively increase of the spirit of research during the past few years than in the study of Psychology, Concentration and Mental Discipline. The requests for authentic lessons in Thought Control, Mental Discipline and... New Age/Business Pages 422

The Lesser Key Of Solomon Goetia *by L. W. de Laurence* ISBN: *1-59462-092-X* **$9.95**
This translation of the first book of the "Lernegton" which is now for the first time made accessible to students of Talismanic Magic was done, after careful collation and edition, from numerous Ancient Manuscripts in Hebrew, Latin, and French... New Age/Occult Pages 92

Rubaiyat Of Omar Khayyam *by Edward Fitzgerald* ISBN:*1-59462-332-5* **$13.95**
Edward Fitzgerald, whom the world has already learned, in spite of his own efforts to remain within the shadow of anonymity, to look upon as one of the rarest poets of the century, was born at Bredfield, in Suffolk, on the 31st of March, 1809. He was the third son of John Purcell... Music Pages 172

Ancient Law *by Henry Maine* ISBN: *1-59462-128-4* **$29.95**
The chief object of the following pages is to indicate some of the earliest ideas of mankind, as they are reflected in Ancient Law, and to point out the relation of those ideas to modern thought. Religiom/History Pages 452

Far-Away Stories *by William J. Locke* ISBN: *1-59462-129-2* **$19.45**
"Good wine needs no bush, but a collection of mixed vintages does. And this book is just such a collection. Some of the stories I do not want to remain buried for ever in the museum files of dead magazine-numbers an author's not unpardonable vanity..." Fiction Pages 272

Life of David Crockett *by David Crockett* ISBN: *1-59462-250-7* **$27.45**
"Colonel David Crockett was one of the most remarkable men of the times in which he lived. Born in humble life, but gifted with a strong will, an indomitable courage, and unremitting perseverance... Biographies/New Age Pages 424

Lip-Reading *by Edward Nitchie* ISBN: *1-59462-206-X* **$25.95**
Edward B. Nitchie, founder of the New York School for the Hard of Hearing, now the Nitchie School of Lip-Reading, Inc, wrote "LIP-READING Principles and Practice". The development and perfecting of this meritorious work on lip-reading was an undertaking... How-to Pages 400

A Handbook of Suggestive Therapeutics, Applied Hypnotism, Psychic Science ISBN: *1-59462-214-0* **$24.95**
by Henry Munro Health/New Age/Health/Self-help Pages 376

A Doll's House: and Two Other Plays *by Henrik Ibsen* ISBN: *1-59462-112-8* **$19.95**
Henrik Ibsen created this classic when in revolutionary 1848 Rome. Introducing some striking concepts in playwriting for the realist genre, this play has been studied the world over. Fiction/Classics/Plays 308

The Light of Asia *by sir Edwin Arnold* ISBN: *1-59462-204-3* **$13.95**
In this poetic masterpiece, Edwin Arnold describes the life and teachings of Buddha. The man who was to become known as Buddha to the world was born as Prince Gautama of India but he rejected the worldly riches and abandoned the reigns of power when... Religion/History/Biographies Pages 170

The Complete Works of Guy de Maupassant *by Guy de Maupassant* ISBN: *1-59462-157-8* **$16.95**
"For days and days, nights and nights, I had dreamed of that first kiss which was to consecrate our engagement, and I knew not on what spot I should put my lips..." Fiction/Classics Pages 240

The Art of Cross-Examination *by Francis L. Wellman* ISBN: *1-59462-309-0* **$26.95**
Written by a renowned trial lawyer, Wellman imparts his experience and uses case studies to explain how to use psychology to extract desired information through questioning. How-to/Science/Reference Pages 408

Answered or Unanswered? *by Louisa Vaughan* ISBN: *1-59462-248-5* **$10.95**
Miracles of Faith in China Religion Pages 112

The Edinburgh Lectures on Mental Science (1909) *by Thomas* ISBN: *1-59462-008-3* **$11.95**
This book contains the substance of a course of lectures recently given by the writer in the Queen Street Hall, Edinburgh. Its purpose is to indicate the Natural Principles governing the relation between Mental Action and Material Conditions... New Age/Psychology Pages 148

Ayesha *by H. Rider Haggard* ISBN: *1-59462-301-5* **$24.95**
Verily and indeed it is the unexpected that happens! Probably if there was one person upon the earth from whom the Editor of this, and of a certain previous history, did not expect to hear again... Classics Pages 380

Ayala's Angel *by Anthony Trollope* ISBN: *1-59462-352-X* **$29.95**
The two girls were both pretty, but Lucy who was twenty-one who supposed to be simple and comparatively unattractive, whereas Ayala was credited, as her Bombwhat romantic name might show, with poetic charm and a taste for romance. Ayala when her father died was nineteen... Fiction Pages 484

The American Commonwealth *by James Bryce* ISBN: *1-59462-286-8* **$34.45**
An interpretation of American democratic political theory. It examines political mechanics and society from the perspective of Scotsman James Bryce Politics Pages 572

Stories of the Pilgrims *by Margaret P. Pumphrey* ISBN: *1-59462-116-0* **$17.95**
This book explores pilgrims religious oppression in England as well as their escape to Holland and eventual crossing to America on the Mayflower, and their early days in New England... History Pages 268

www.bookjungle.com *email: sales@bookjungle.com fax: 630-214-0564 mail: Book Jungle PO Box 2226 Champaign, IL 61825*

QTY

The Fasting Cure *by Sinclair Upton* ISBN: *1-59462-222-1* **$13.95**
In the Cosmopolitan Magazine for May, 1910, and in the Contemporary Review (London) for April, 1910, I published an article dealing with my experiences in fasting. I have written a great many magazine articles, but never one which attracted so much attention... New Age/Self Help/Health Pages 164

Hebrew Astrology *by Sepharial* ISBN: *1-59462-308-2* **$13.45**
In these days of advanced thinking it is a matter of common observation that we have left many of the old landmarks behind and that we are now pressing forward to greater heights and to a wider horizon than that which represented the mind-content of our progenitors... Astrology Pages 144

Thought Vibration or The Law of Attraction in the Thought World ISBN: *1-59462-127-6* **$12.95**
by William Walker Atkinson Psychology/Religion Pages 144

Optimism *by Helen Keller* ISBN: *1-59462-108-X* **$15.95**
Helen Keller was blind, deaf, and mute since 19 months old, yet famously learned how to overcome these handicaps, communicate with the world, and spread her lectures promoting optimism. An inspiring read for everyone... Biographies/Inspirational Pages 84

Sara Crewe *by Frances Burnett* ISBN: *1-59462-360-0* **$9.45**
In the first place, Miss Minchin lived in London. Her home was a large, dull, tall one, in a large, dull square, where all the houses were alike, and all the sparrows were alike, and where all the door-knockers made the same heavy sound... Childrens/Classic Pages 88

The Autobiography of Benjamin Franklin *by Benjamin Franklin* ISBN: *1-59462-135-7* **$24.95**
The Autobiography of Benjamin Franklin has probably been more extensively read than any other American historical work, and no other book of its kind has had such ups and downs of fortune. Franklin lived for many years in England, where he was agent... Biographies/History Pages 332

Name	
Email	
Telephone	
Address	
City, State ZIP	

☐ **Credit Card**   ☐ **Check / Money Order**

Credit Card Number	
Expiration Date	
Signature	

Please Mail to: Book Jungle
PO Box 2226
Champaign, IL 61825
or Fax to: 630-214-0564

ORDERING INFORMATION
web*: www.bookjungle.com*
email*: sales@bookjungle.com*
fax*: 630-214-0564*
mail*: Book Jungle PO Box 2226 Champaign, IL 61825*
or PayPal *to sales@bookjungle.com*

Please contact us for bulk discounts

DIRECT-ORDER TERMS
20% Discount if You Order Two or More Books
Free Domestic Shipping!
Accepted: Master Card, Visa, Discover, American Express

www.ingramcontent.com/pod-product-compliance
Lightning Source LLC
Chambersburg PA
CBHW081232090426
42738CB00016B/3274